Dieter Graf

Santorini
Sifnos
Western & Southern
Cyclades

Anáfi
Folégandros
Ios
Kéa
Kímolos
Kíthnos
Mílos
Santoríni
  & Thirassía
Sérifos
Sífnos
Síkinos

Hiking and Swimming for Island Hoppers
51 Walks on 12 Greek Islands

Graf Editions

Using this illustrated walking guide

AWT stands for Actual Walking Time. This time does not include breaks, wrong turns or sight-seeing. The AWT serves as a personal control as to whether certain route markings, emphasized in **bold print,** have been reached in the given time. These times are an aid for orientation and should not be considered as encouragement to achieve a record performance. Spot heights are added in brackets.

The approximate **overall length** of a walk is specified in hours in the introduction to each tour. These figures do not include time taken for bus trips or extra-long breaks. Information concerning the **length of the walks**, the **difference in altitude** and three **levels of difficulty** can also be found there.

Route photos are intended for orientation, for consulting locals and as a stimulus. The corresponding text is marked by 1 to 4.

The **route sketches** have been drawn to the best of our knowledge but lay no claim to completeness. GPS points are shown as P in texts and on maps. Map datum WGS84. We would be grateful for information concerning **changes** in paths and similar data. As a token of our appreciation we will send you a free copy of our next edition. Updates can be found on the Internet.

The author Dieter Graf is an architect who has travelled all over the world. He has walked the Aegean Islands since the years when tourism was just beginning there and is considered a connoisseur of the islands.

© 2006 Edition Dieter Graf, Elisabethstr. 29, 80796 Muenchen, Germany
Tel. 0049-(0)89-271 59 57, Fax 0049-(0)89-271 59 97
www.graf-editions.de

All rights reserved.

Type-Setting: Michael Henn, Ottobrunn
Maps: Kurt Zucher, Starnberg
Translation: Myles Oliver

Original Title: „Wandern auf Griechischen Inseln: Santorin, Sifnos, Westliche und Suedliche Kykladen" (ISBN 3-9808802-2-2)

Cover Photo: Santoríni, chapel near Oía

ISBN 3-9808802-3-0

Contents

Tips for Walks *6*
Landscape, Flora, Fauna *10*
History *15*
Translation Helper F, I, NL, S *19*
Walks *20*
Island Hopping *191*
Explanation of Symbols *192*

Islands	Walks	Page
Santoríni & Thirassía	① ② ③ ④ ⑤ ⑥ ⑦ ⑧ ⑨	20
Sífnos	⑩ ⑪ ⑫ ⑬ ⑭ ⑮ ⑯ ⑰ ⑱ ⑲ ⑳ ㉑	46
Anáfi	㉒ ㉓ ㉔	86
Folégandros	㉕ ㉖ ㉗	96
Ios	㉘ ㉙ ㉚	107
Kéa	㉛ ㉜ ㉝ ㉞	118
Kímolos	㉟ ㊱ ㊲	131
Kíthnos	㊳ ㊴ ㊵	141
Mílos	㊶ ㊷ ㊸ ㊹	151
Sérifos	㊺ ㊻ ㊼ ㊽	166
Síkinos	㊾ ㊿ 51	180

Sífnos, Panagía tosou neróu

The Western and Southern Cyclades

The concept "Greek Islands" conjures up images of white cubical houses twined around with red bougainvillea, unevenly paved alleys below bright blue church domes, dilapidated windmills on top of stormy mountain ridges, shady groves with old gnarled olive trees.

The Cyclades fit this picture perfectly. The name of this group of islands is derived from the classical Greek word *kyklos*, meaning "circle". The ancient Greeks believed that the islands were gathered in a circle round the holy island of Délos.

The western and southern Cyclades described in this book used to be classed with the Sporades, the "scattered islands", but nowadays they are considered part of the Cyclades on account of their many common features in terms of history and culture. Cycladic culture in the early Bronze Age was the first very advanced civilisation in Europe. During the subsequent classical period the first stone temples were also built here. One of the aims of this book is to discover these on walks. Along the trails described here are old Byzantine fortified monasteries as well as tightly clustered villages and long since deserted, solitary farmhouses. Readers are also led to long sandy beaches and concealed rocky bays which can only be reached on foot.

The Cyclades offer a wonderful, tranquil landscape. Even the barrenness has its charm. The walker's eye is rewarded with distant views of the blue sea from almost every point along the way. Moreover, his nose is tickled by the sweet smells of the Mediterranean kitchen herbs which thrive everywhere. In the villages, finally, his heart warms to the *filoxénia*, the generous hospitality of the Greeks which makes one forget that one is a foreigner.

The islands are still criss-crossed by many of the old mule tracks, which connect the traditional settlements and now frequently abandoned monasteries. Fences are rare, too, so trekkers are more or less free to roam wherever they want. Although each of the islands has its own specific characterisitcs, Sífnos and Kéa are particularly suitable for walking, closely followed by Síkinos and Sérifos. But each trekker can decide that for himself; sooner or later everyone finds his or her "favourite" island.

Have a good trip   *Kaló taxídi*!

Walking the Greek Islands

The Greek countryside is one of the loveliest hiking areas in Europe. One reason is the old mule tracks, the **monopátia** (sing. monopáti). For hundreds of years they were used by the farmers' beasts of burden. Wider paths, the **kalderími**, connected larger villages and served as paths for pilgrims to the monasteries. They were paved with marble, bordered with walls and suitable only for man and animal.

Our times have torn this net of paths apart by broadening the mule tracks to make them accessible to cars wherever it seemed to be necessary and by pushing aside the characteristic dry walls along the waysides, all financed by money from the European Union Regional Funds. The remaining paths are now superfluous and in ruins and are gradually being forgotten by the inhabitants. This book aims to help ensure that the old mule tracks which still exist are used again and hence preserved before they are irreparably destroyed. Wherever still intact, they are described in this book. Meanwhile, incidentally, the new EU "Leader" Fund sets out among other things to preserve the remaining network of paths.

The routes described have been walked along again shortly before publication and can be followed without difficulty by people in normal **physical condition**; special surefootedness is not necessary. The (arrow)✓ markings in the text concern only those who are very afraid of heights. Some of the walks are suitable for children. For longer walking tours **short cuts** are indicated.

A few **tips** for wandering: in order to get your blood circulation going, you should begin leisurely for the first fifteen minutes and then continue at the speed that is right for you, where you breathe only through your nose. It is important to eat and especially to drink often, even if you don't feel the need to do so.

Mule dung on the narrow paths is more certain to lead you further than goat droppings since the goat paths usually end somewhere in the scrub, while mules always return to their stalls.

Steel mesh used as grazing fences can best be climbed over with the help of a pile of stones or at a spot where the "barbs" on top can be turned down most easily. If necessary, wire fences can be opened at the joints and then shut again. Pasture fences are knotted shut on the side where there are two perpendicular rods. You owe it to the farmers whose land you walk across to shut the openings again afterwards, of course. Access to the sea is allowed in Greece as a matter of principle. Due to the good views, the tours normally lead from the mountains to the sea – so take along your swimming gear.

You should be absolutely sure to pick a nice day for tours in the mountains since there is always the danger of sudden fog formation. Then the few markings aren't of much help. If you want to walk alone, you should by all means leave information in your hotel.

On some islands there is an increased risk of forest fires in the summer. For this reason no inflammable objects or pieces of glass should be thrown away along the trail.

No liability can be assumed for accidents along the walking routes suggested or for possible civil law demands by landowners. Nor can a guarantee be given for bus schedules or opening times. The website www.graf-editions.de can inform you of any changes that occur along walking routes.

Coloured dots and arrows can often be found as **markings along paths**, but they do not necessarily correspond to the descriptions in this book.

Red-and-white metal signs with numbers are new and have been put up by domestic organisations. If you have orientation problems, you should always ask the locals about the "monopáti", otherwise you will be directed to roads for vehicular traffic.

For some of the islands there are road maps from freytag&bernd, Greek Road Editions and recently good Greek maps from the Anavasi publishing house. Other Greek maps are not suitable for walking tours.

Almost all the starting and finishing points are served by public **buses**, even in the low season. In case a service does not operate on Sundays, take a **taxi**. You should always make a point of settling the price before you begin the trip. The taximeter is only turned on when you specifically request it. The relatively high price is considered a surcharge for the poor stretches of road. You can arrange with the driver at which spot you want to be picked up later or phone for a taxi along the way. This usually works out well. Another possibility for circular walking tours is a relatively reasonable rental car or a rental motor bike. In addition, car drivers also enjoy taking along a wanderer who waves him down.

Despite countermeasures **environmental protection** still remains an unsolved problem, so some things you see lying around while walking through the countryside will not always correspond to your sense of order and environmental stipulations. The Greek remains true to his character: he is also very generous with his garbage.

Walking   7

Appropriate **hiking gear** includes a backpack for a day, shoes with good soles (no sandals), comfortable socks, long trousers or zipper trousers*, possibly a mobile phone, binoculars, a whistle, a small flashlight and picnic equipment (with salt-shaker). In the spring and autumn, rainwear is a necessity. A compass would also be good, but is not necessary if you have a fairly good sense of orientation.

*The legs of zipper trousers which also have vertical zippers can be zipped together to form a pad to sit on at the beach. And if you connect both zippers, you have a chic skirt for visiting monasteries.

Climate and Walking Seasons

The typical temperate Mediterranean climate with a hot summer and a mild rainy winter predominates on the Cyclades. The maximum air temperature is 32° C in August (at night 22° C). In winter the temperature sinks to 15° C (7° C) in February. On mountains above 1000 m snow can fall every 3–4 years and lie for a short while.

The water temperatures are lowest in February at 16° C and reach an almost subtropical 25° C in August. You can go swimming from the end of May at 19° C through to October (22° C). The rainy days are spread irregularly throughout the year. Most of the rain falls in December and January, when it rains on about 14 days. You must still calculate with 3 days of rain in May, while there is absolute dryness from June to August. Statistically October again has 6 days of rain, but it is not very plentiful.

The number of hours of sunshine per day corresponds to this pattern. In December and January the very strong winter sun only shines for about 4.5 hours. Even in May the wanderer must reconcile himself to 10.1 hours of sunshine per day and the swimmer to 12.1 in August. October is once again pleasant for autumn walkers, with 7.8 hours of sunshine per day.

Strong north winds are characteristic of the Aegean Islands, with three to four Beaufort on a yearly average. One reason for this is the difference in air pressure between the Azore highs and the hot low pressure areas above the Persian Gulf. In the transition season, especially in April and May and then October and November, the Boréas dominates, a cool, wet north wind. In the summer (May to September) the famous etesien winds, called the meltémia, often blow for days under a cloudless blue sky,

8 Cyclades

regularly strong from north to northeast, with velocities of five to six Beaufort. The sky can then be somewhat overcast. Towards evening the meltémi usually slackens somewhat, but it can also blow with considerable strength for days on end.

The sirocco occurs less frequently, but especially in spring. It comes from the hot Sahara desert, picking up moisture over the Mediterranean to bring the Aegean warm humidity from the south.

On the Greek islands there are several different seasons for walking tours. Anyone wishing to feast his eyes should plan his tour around Easter. It might be somewhat cool and even muddy, but the countryside is grass-green, poppy-red and broom-yellow; the houses and alleyways are freshly whitewashed. The preparations for the Greek Easter celebration alone make the trip worthwhile. However, you can't go swimming yet, and some hotels and tavernas are still closed. In April it can rain briefly. The Greeks divide the year into three parts, and this one is called "the time of blossoming and maturing".

In May and June the blossom time is already partially over, but, since it is very warm and the number of tourists is still limited, this is probably the most attractive time for walking. Beginning at the end of May the water has a pleasant temperature.

The main tourist season in July and August is not highly recommended for walking tours due to the heat. It is the "dry period" in Greece. The dry north winds, which blow continuously, still make the temperatures bearable, but at noon it is wise to seek a shady spot under a tree. Harvest time begins in July. On 15th August, the Assumption of the Virgin, called "Passing Away Peacefully" in the Eastern Church, there are great celebrations everywhere with roast lamb, music and dance.

From the beginning of September on, the heat is over and the sea still has a pleasant temperature for swimming, up until the end of October. Now it is again possible to take longer walking tours, but only until about 6 pm due to the shorter period of daylight. The land has become yellow and brown, the fields bear their fruit, and everywhere you meet friendly farmers harvesting their last crops. From the beginning of October on, it can start to rain again. The restaurants and hotels gradually shut down and some owners travel to their winter residences in Athens. Others put on camouflage suits, reach for their guns and search through the undergrowth. A million Greeks are passionate hunters. In November there is usually a change in climate, with heavy rainfall. Then it becomes unpleasant. The period from November to

Climate 9

February is called the "rain season". Although there are some warm, sunny days around Christmas, it is more pleasant at home.

Geology

The northern Aegean was not flooded by the sea until after the last Ice Age. Up until then the present island arc between Crete and Rhodes formed the southern edge of the mainland.

The more northern Cycladic islands stand on a submarine mountain which was raised out of the sea 50 million years ago by the pressure of the African continental plate on the European continental plate. After repeated rising and subsiding the islands assumed their current form. That is why one encounters slate, a sedimentary rock which was lifted out of the sea and sits on top of a bed of marble and granite. If the pressure exerted on the European continental plate persists, this will ultimately lead to the islands being lifted further out of the sea and, after about 50 million years, the Mediterranean sea disappearing altogether. Then there will be a land connection between Africa, Asia and Europe. On the southern edge of the Aegean an active seismic arc extends from the Peleponnesus via the islands Póros, Mílos, Santoríni, Anáfi, Níssiros and Kos as far as the Taurus mountain range in Turkey. The pressure created by the land masses discharges itself here now and again as earthquakes. Half the earthquakes in Europe occur in Greece, which in addition has dormant, but also active volcanoes such as on Mílos and above all on Santoríni. These southern islands consist of volcanic tuff and lava resting on older, non-volcanic rocks.

Fauna

As a result of the mostly low vegetation large game is not encountered. The animals one most often comes across are goats and sheep, though not in such large numbers as in former years. Hares and martens are rare.

Along the way you frequently see the small common lizard, which can be up to 10 cm long. The dragon-like agama (hardun) ①, its bigger relative, is up to 30 cm long.

The careful wanderer will rarely see snakes. There is only one poisonous type: the horn or sand viper (vipera ammodytes

meridionalis) 2. It can be up to 50 cm long and as thick as two thumbs. A healthy adult hardly need fear a deadly bite.

The non-poisonous sand-boa is about the same size; it lives in very concealed spots. The non-poisonous four-striped adder reaches an adult length of more than a metre and a width almost as thick as an arm. Its size is frightening, but it is harmless, as is the ring-snake.

Scorpions reaching a size of up to 5 cm also live here. A bite is rather painful but not deadly. They love to hide in shoes.

Land turtles 3 have now become rare. You can rouse crabs, frogs and eels along the watercourses which carry water all year round. Monk seals live on the island of Poliégos near Mílos.

Flora

Along with Spain, Greece has the greatest variety of plants in Europe. Nevertheless, ever since antiquity forests on the Aegean islands have been cut down for building ships or have become

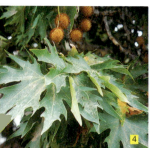  

victims of forest fires in summer, causing some parts of the countryside to seem like karstland. This effect is intensified by the limestone soil which cannot store water.

The stock of trees consists mainly of aleppo pines 1, from which the resin for retsina wine is obtained. Taller evergreen oaks and kermes oaks 2 grow in protected regions which are rich in water. Unassuming, salt-tolerant tamarisks 3 are found along beaches. Plane-trees 4 shade the village squares and slender cypresses the cemeteries. Acacias, poplars, alders, maples and eucalyptus trees 5 can also be found, as well as mulberry trees 6 and carobs 7. Among the fruit trees there are pomegranates, fig trees 8 and citrus fruits. Yet dominating the landscape most of all is the olive tree, which looks strangely deformed as it gets older.

On slopes and mountain tops, dry shrubs reaching a height of up to half a metre predominate, thorny undergrowth called phrýgana in Greek. Typical representatives of this "low macchia" are broom, thorny knap-weed (centauria spinosa), heather, spiny spurge plants (euphorbia) 9 10, plants often shaped like hedgehogs.

12 **Cyclades**

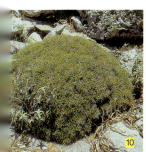  

Thicker bush or tree groups up to two metres high with evergreens and bushes with hard leaves are not found as frequently. This "high macchia" is called xerovumi in Greek. Kermes oaks with serrated leaves ②, juniper and mastic bushes ⑪ are particularly predominant. Mastic bushes are used for manufacturing rubber and raki spirits.

The keeping of goats has caused the beginnings of higher vegetation to be kept low. Sometimes even grazing land is burned in order to give the goats the freshly growing sprouts as food. Inedible plants such as Jerusalem sage, squill or asphodel ⑫ grow here quickly.

Agaves (agave americana) ⑬ often line the lanes and paths. This thorny leaf plant has only grown in the Mediterranean area since the 16th century. Fig-cactus ⑭, with its thorny but tasty fruit, is also widespread.

A surprisingly abundant splendour of flowers appears in the spring. Already in January the anemone and crocus blossom. From February to April white and red blossoming rockroses ⑮, iris, yellow daffodils, hyacinths, lupines, chrysanthemums and

Flora   13

broom add magic to the landscape with their cheery colours, and the poppy adds its bright red.

Small orchids are an adornment of spring for a short time. The bee orchid (ophrys) [16], lax-flowered orchid (orchis), tongue orchid (serapias) and dragon arum [17] can be seen frequently.

In May and June the main blossoming season comes to an end, but summer doesn't mean brown wilderness by any means. Bougainvillea radiates its bright colours on the house walls, and oleander blossoms in moist spots. The thorny acanthus [18] and the gold thistle [19] bloom along the wayside.

In the late summer and autumn the flora begins to come alive again and blossom after the first brief rain showers. Meadow-saffron, heather and squill reveal themselves along with the crocus-like stellaria bergia, dandelions, thistles and cyclamen.

Many of the plants contain ethereal oils. In the heat of the day you can especially appreciate the pleasantly spicy aroma of thyme, rosemary, lavender, oregano, camomile and fennel. Sage [20], capers [21] and other kitchen herbs often border the walking paths.

Historical Data

The Cyclades have been settled since the Mesolithic period (7500 BC). Traces of settlements dating back to the end of the 4th millennium BC have been proven at Korissía on Kéa and on the small island of Sáliegos near Páros. This is when the obsidian export from Mílos begins, the hard black volcanic rock serving to make tools. The first immigrants, the Carians, come from Asia Minor around 2800 BC. The islands' position between Europe and Asia makes them a bridge between the cultures and one of the oldest landscapes in Europe to be cultivated very early.

During the transition from the Stone Age to the Bronze Age Europe experiences its first artistic climax, the Cycladic culture (3200–1100 BC). The flat female figures with folded arms made of marble are famous. The creators of these up to 1.50 m high idols strongly influenced Mycenaean art.

Four thousand years ago the Phoenicians arrive from the coast of what is now Lebanon. They impart the skills of the Assyrians and Babylonians to the Greeks, as well as introducing writing and money. They are interested in trade rather than colonization. Then the islands come under the influence of Minoan Crete, which establishes settlements on Santoríni and Mílos. Around 1650 BC the volcanic eruption on Santoríni destroys much of what man has so far created.

Following the decline of the Cretan palaces around 1450 BC Mycenaean settlers from the Peleponnesus land and dictate subsequent events. On the mainland the Indo-European Dorians immigrating from the north later trigger a migration of peoples. After 1100 BC the islands of the Aegean and Asia Minor are colonized from there in several waves. The northern Cyclades are dominated by the Ionians, while the southern islands are later ruled by the spartan Dorians.

Archaic Period   (800–500 v. Chr.) The Ionians are the first to release the Greek spirit in the sense of artistic, intellectual and economic freedom. In the sixth century BC the leadership of Greek culture is found on the islands. The mainland does not adopt these ideas until later. In terms of architecture it seems that stone temples were built on the islands much earlier.

Starting in 540 BC, the Persian Empire extends its influence to the coast of Asia Minor. Athens takes a stand and makes Délos the intellectual and cultural centre of the Attic-Delian maritime alliance. This protective league against Persia unites the Greeks in the Aegean and Asia Minor with Athens. War is unavoidable and begins in 490 BC.

The Classical Period   (490–336 BC) Some Dorian islands fight on the side of the enemy at the beginning of the Persian Wars, but they, too, are on Athens' side for the final triumph over the Persians in 449 BC. Immense riches are amassed on Délos during the "Golden Age" which follows. When Athens carries off the treasure and tries to make vassals of its allies, the latter fight against Athens in allegiance to Sparta in the Peloponnesian War, that lasts 30 years. The outcome is a forever weakened Greece. Athens loses all its importance.

Hellenistic Period   (338–146 BC) The Macedonians in northern Greece take over Greek culture after conquering Greece in 338 BC. For a short period Alexander the Great, a Macedonian, takes this culture, henceforth known as "Hellenism", as far as India. After his early death his world empire rapidly disintegrates into Diadochean empires, the Aegean islands being dominated by the Egyptian Ptolemies.

Roman Period   (146 BC–395 AD) After 146 BC the Romans, as the next rulers, also make Greek culture their own, thus helping it to spread throughout Europe. Greek culture becomes that of the Occident. From Rome comes Christianity, which also becomes the state religion in the Eastern Roman Empire after 391. Already before that there were Christian communities hidden away, for example on Mílos.

The Byzantine Period   (395–1543 AD) The Roman Empire is divided in 395 AD. While the Western Roman Empire is in decline after the migration of peoples in 476 AD, the eastern part of the Imperium Romanum remains an upholder of Graeco-Roman culture for 1000 years. Byzantium, the second Rome, turns eastwards, brings Christianity to the Slavs and spreads Greek ideas as far as Moscow, which later becomes known as the Second Byzantium or Third Rome. The new Islamic ideas also influence Greece in the 8th and 9th centuries. The iconoclastic controversy revolves around the admissibility of a pictorial representation of God and the Saints. The image worshipers prevail.
Europe begins to drift apart in cultural terms; the religious differences also deepen. The main points of dispute concern the Holy Ghost and the corporeal ascension of Mary, which is considered

as a "peaceful passing away" in the Orthodox Church. The popes dislike the way the Byzantine Emperor is head of the church. In 1054 the schism, or final separation of the Eastern Greek-Orthodox Church from the Western Latin Church, comes about.

In these uncertain times the islands of the Aegean are often attacked by raiders such as the Vandals, the Goths, the Normans and finally the Saracens. The inhabitants of the islands withdraw into the mountain villages. It isn't until the 9th century that Byzantium can consolidate its power once again.

Now, however, in the wake of the Persians, Avars and Arabs, a new Asian power has assembled on the eastern borders of Byzantium: the Turkish Seljuks. They push westward with immense force. In 1095 the Eastern Roman Empire requests help from Pope Urban II, and the crusades begin. They are a fiasco. During the fourth crusade one of the most short-sighted campaigns in history is initiated. Due to trade rivalries Venice induces the crusaders to plunder and occupy the Byzantine capital, Constantinople, in 1204. The quadriga on San Marco square is part of the loot. Not until 1261 do the Byzantians conquer the city again with the aid of the Genoans, thus terminating the Venetians' "Latin Empire". Byzantium is too weak to ever recover again and is conquered by the Turks in 1453.

The Era of the Knights (1204–1537) For most of the islands Venetian domination begins after the sack of Constantinople. They are handed over to the influential Venetian families as fiefs. But the Turkish-Ottoman Empire directs all its energy towards conquering Europe. After the fall of Rhodes, the strongest fortress of Christianity, in 1523, the Turks push on further west. In 1537 they conquer all the Cycladic islands apart from Tínos.

The Turkish Era (1537–1830) The Fall of Constantinople marks the end of the thousand-year-old advanced Roman-Greek civilization. Learned Byzantine fugitives bring the Greek way of thinking back to the West again, paving the way for the Renaissance. From this time on the fortune of the Orthodox Church is determined in Moscow, which assumes the Byzantine double-headed eagle as its state coat of arms.

Yet in Greece itself the Turkish influence, from diet to music, predominates for the next 350 years. This influence is still discernible today. The Orthodox Church is recognised by the Turks as a mediator between government and population and proves to be the protector of Greek culture during this period.

History 17

Russian Pan-Slavism under Catherine the Great seeks to release the Balkan Slavs from the Turkish sphere and bring them into the Russian fold. The Turkish-Russian war of 1768 to 1774 extends as far as the Aegean, where a Russian fleet occupies 18 Cycladic islands for four years; they later return to Turkish rule.

Independent Greece (since 1821) In 1821 the insurrection against the Turks begins on the Peloponnesus as Turkey has been weakened after another war against Russia. Europe reflects on its cultural roots. The political stability of post-Napoleonic Europe and Classicism in art increase an awareness of eastern Europe. Philhellenists from many countries support the Greek struggle for independence, the Great Powers in Europe help diplomatically, and Greece becomes part of Europe again.
The Cyclades are part of Greece from the outset, unlike the islands off the Turkish coast. They remain Turkish and are under Italian rule from 1912 until 1943.

Twentieth Century Greece tries to regain possession of its former settlements from the "sick man on the Bosporus". During the 1912–13 Balkan wars and the First World War several islands and Ottoman areas on the northern coast of the Aegean are occupied. After the First World War, among whose losers is Turkey, the opportunity appears favourable again. The Greeks start a war over the former areas in Asia Minor. But Turkey, emboldened once again by the "Young Turk Revolution", utterly destroys the Greeks, who then have to agree to a major population exchange. In 1940 fascist Italy vainly attempts to occupy the country, whereupon German troops advance across the Balkans to Greece. They hand the country over to the Italians as occupied territory, but then occupy it themselves after Mussolini's fall in 1943, remaining on many islands until the end of the war.

After World War II With Western help during the civil war from 1945 to 1949, Greece avoids the fate of the other Balkan countries, and doesn't disappear behind the Iron Curtain. Gradually Greece is accepted in most important European institutions. European subsidies lead to an improvement in the infrastructure and facilitate a growth in tourism, which becomes the most important economic sector in the country. The drachma, the oldest currency in the world, is replaced by the euro in 2002.

Translation of special words for hikers

English	Français	Italiano	Nederlands	Svenska
boulder	bloc de rocher	masso	Rotsblok	klippblock
cairn	marquage	segnalato di pietre	Markeringssteen	vägmärke
cleft	fossé	fosso	Sloot	sänka
crest	crête	dorsale	Bergkam	bergskam
culvert	caniveau	passagio	water buis	vattenledning
defile	défilé	strada incassata	holleweg	hålväg
dirt road	chemin rural	sentiero di camp.	Onverharde weg	åkerväg
dip	dépression	depressione	Glooiing	sänka
ditch	fossé	fosso	Sloot	sänka
ford	gué	guado	doorwaadbare Pl.	vadställe
fork	bifurcation	bifurcazione	Wegsplitsing	vägskäl
furrow	fossé	fosso	Sloot	grav
gap	brèche	breccia	Bres	inskärning
clearing	clairière	radura	Open plek in bos	glänta
gorge	gorge	abisso	Kloof	ravin
gravel	pierraille	ghiaia	Steengruis	stenskärvor
grove	bosquet	bosco	Bosschage	lund
gully	cours d'eau	letto di fiume	Waterloop	vattendrag
heath	bruyère	brughiera	Heide	hed
hollow	dépression	depressione	Glooiing	sänka
incline	pente	pendio	Helling	sluttning
incision	fossé	fosso	Sloot	sänka
juniper	genévrier	ginepro	jeneverstruik	enbuske
past	près de	accanto a	naast	jämte
pebble	caillou	ciottolo	Kiezel	grus
pen	bergerie	stalla ovile	Stal	stall
ravine	ravin	abisso	Ravijn	ravin
rim	bords	orlo	Rand	kant
ridge	crête	cresta	Bergkam	bergskam
rubble	éboulis	ditriti	Steengruis	stenar
saddle	crête	sella	Bergrug	bergsrygg
schist	schiste	scisto	leisteen	skiffer
scree	éboulis	ditriti	Steengruis	stenar
scrub	fourré	sterpaglia	Doornbos	snår
slope	pente	pendio	Helling	sluttning
stream-bed	lit	letto di fiume	Waterloop	vattendrag
strenuous	fatigant	faticoso	inspannend	ansträngande
trail	piste	sentiero	Pad	stig
turn off	bifurcation	biforcazione	Afslag	avtagsväg
well	puits	pozzo	Bron	brunn

Santoríni

The very dry and, in summer, hot volcanic island is quite unlike the other Cyclades. Its present-day appearance dates back to the eruption of a volcano beneath the originally round limestone island about 1600 BC. This was the greatest catastrophe in the history of mankind. An up to 60 metre thick layer of pumice tuff ejected by the eruption was deposited on what remained of the island. In this layer are now found the typical valleys formed by erosion, with their cave dwellings. The island has a good network of roads and tracks for farmers and tourists, thus making it somewhat difficult to find secluded trails. Shady trees are rare; the landscape is dominated by vineyards. Santoríni is characterised by its lower-level mule tracks bordered by black lava stones and sand, as fine as icing sugar. The bus connections are reliable and serve the start and end of all the walks described.
Walking tours 1 and 6 are particularly recommended.

Thirassía

This is the other remnant of the volcanic catastrophe: the former western edge of the sunken island of Strongli, "the circular one" (see left). The island has remained pastoral, tourism never having established itself here. Currently there is not even a place to stay overnight, so only day trips can be considered.
For both islands good maps have been produced by Anavasi, Karto-Atelier (Switzerland) and Road Editions on scale 1:35 000 to 1:40 000.

❶ Cliffhanger

This is the classical Santoríni trek: three hours along the verge of a precipice with spectacular views and a wonderful picnic spot!
■ *9 km, altitude difference 130 m, easy to moderate*

AWT
0.00
0.05

If you don't want to arrive in Oía until sunset, it will do to start walking at 2 pm. The tour begins at the Archaeological **Museum** of **Fíra** and leads past the well known vantage points – the first of which is **Fírostefani** –, then on past the large convent Agios Nikoláos (tour possible) to **Imerovígli**. From the end of that village 1 we take the dirt track along the edge of the crater. Beyond a hollow, where there is a graveyard, the track climbs gently before

0.55

forking at a hotel complex. Our subsequent main route continues along to the right.

★

Down to the left it only takes five minutes to reach **St. Antonius Chapel** *2, a resting place the like of which is seldom encountered on the Cyclades. Everything is already prepared for us: picnic tables, a cool cave, a tap and even a WC hut.*

The island of Volcano, which rose up from the almost 400 m deep caldera a mere 300 years ago, lies peacefully in the centre of the crater. This landscape was formed by the largest natural catastrophe in the history of mankind. The volcano, originally 1600 m high, erupted around 1600 BC, then caved in, destroying in one fell swoop Théra civilization on Strongili – "the circular one", as the island was then known.

Reluctantly, we leave this belvedere and climb back up to

22   Santoríni

the main track, where we continue on past a dilapidated church. Almost on the summit of the mountain stands
1.10 the church of **Profítis Elías** ③. Having walked down a stony, yet easy path alongside the precipice, you come to
1.20 a **road**, which should be followed for just 250 m.

At the cantina, known for its freshly-squeezed oranges, is an attractive mule track leading uphill to Negolo Vounó.
1.45 A **chapel** with a superb view of the northern part of Santoríni awaits us on the next peak. The way now continues down over lava to the village Finikía, past another chapel ④, which this time bears the name of the prophet Elias.

> *Alternative:* Those still wishing to go for a **swim** should cross over the hill 250 m beyond the chapel of Elias, heading downhill to the right of the water tank, across the road and into the tranquil village of **Finikía** and from there, next to an overgrown footpath, out of the eroded valley and straight on to the sea. To get from here to Oía, you follow the descriptions in (②, in the opposite direction).

On the outskirts of Oía do not be put off by the rumbling
2.05 sounds emanating from the **desalination plant**, for this is where the refreshing water for our shower comes from. Heading on over a hillside path, past enticing swimming pools, we come to the road next to the "Oía Market" and follow it for a short stretch. We bear left up the steps from
2.10 the **Church of St. George** and cross the churchyard to the main road through Oía. A few minutes along to the right is the taverna "Blue Sky", which offers a magnificent view back along the way we have just come. Later we follow the stream of tourists heading, like us, along the main road to "Sunset Point".

Fíra – Oía 23

24 Santoríni

❷ Beachcomber

A hike for beachcombers! Starting from Oía, we wander along the east coast, past many attractive bathing places, in six hours. But a strenuous 40 minute climb awaits us at the end. The trek can be broken off in Imerovígli.
■ *13 km, difference in altitude 290 m, difficult*

▷ *Map see left*

AWT 0.00 — This trek begins to the right of the dustbins, opposite the "**Oía Market**" ①, where you go down the narrow concrete track beside the car park. Later on you may have trouble with the broken stones, but not with your orientation. The path leads through vineyards towards the sea; part of it has to be circumnavigated. Heading left along the next dirt track, and turning off it to the right after 200 m, will bring you straight to the taverna "Paradisos"

0.30 — on the **road**. Here you have three taverns to choose from, or you can proceed straight on down to the black-and-white **Baxedes Beach**, shuffling through the sand and drifting on in a northerly direction.

1.00 — Soon you find yourself alone with the bizarrely shaped pumice cliffs ②. Dotted along the beach are a few **tamarisks** – perhaps you're lucky and the places in the shade are still free. Further on the bow of **Cape Koloúmpos** heaves into the sea ③, but you now have to scramble up

1.20 — to the right, over fallen dry-stone walls, to the **marker post**. Up above is the mountain of Kókkino Voúno, down below in the sea Amorgós, Astipálea and Anáfi are lined

Oía – Póri – Imerovígli – Fíra

up like pearls – and all around is the scent of thyme.
We then use the street for a few metres, before going down to the left through the bed of a stream, back to the strand with all its jetsam – perfect for the beachcomber! A row of windmills, which we will pass later on, is visible on the hill ahead ④. Perched above the coastline are the houses of Póri. Using some steps in the red cliffs, we reach
1.55 a small **fishing port**, where Capt. Jannis' cantina awaits our arrival. (**P**: N 36°27.567'/ E 25°25.746')
We continue up to the main road, cross it and head on without any trail, accompanied by prickly pears, along the foot of the mountain as far as the windmills. After so-
2.10 me houses we come across **two chapels**.
On closer inspection the "windmills" turn out to be unfinished buildings, intended as holiday homes. A steep ascent commences above the water tank belonging to the next residential complex. Bearing *slightly* to the left, it is necessary to struggle uphill without any trail, through tangled scrub, as far as the road leading upwards, which
2.45 eventually comes to the **main road**. On the other side of the road a well worn trail leads over the mountain ridge
2.55 to the **route along the crater**.
The effort is worth it, for the view is spectacular. If you go left, you pass some hotels and arrive on the outskirts of
3.15 **Imerovígli**. Here you could take the bus. Alternatively, you can fortify yourself and enjoy the magnificent panorama. Towering above the sea used to be the Venetian kástro. Stroll along the "promenade", past **Fírostefani**
3.50 with its quiet, attractive eateries, to **Fíra**.

26   **Santoríni**

❸ Erosion

The eroded valleys, almost as typical of Santoríni as the caldera precipice, are little known. From the fortress in Pírgos you have a view over the largest of these valleys. Our route is quickly planned: we will climb down into the next valley, wander through the gorge near Vothónas towards the airport and on to bathe in Kamarí. It should not take more than two-and-a-half to three hours.
■ *7 km, difference in altitude 365 m, easy*

AWT The Perissa bus takes you to **Pírgos**, the capital of the island until 1800. Take a stroll through the old, winding lanes up to the Venetian fortress. Here your gaze can roam far over Santoríni. Before descending, you should note the conspicuously intrusive concrete factory below the town, facing in the direction of Fíra, as you will be passing it later on.

0.00 Below the fortress is a small **obelisk** – a military memorial. You walk north in the lane below and come across a church ① 50 m further on. The path leads downhill from here, under a flying buttress and right at the fork down to a concrete ramp which joins a road. Going right along it for 40 m, you take another concrete ramp down to the left. Later the ramp will become a clean, plastered winegrowers' path, sunk in to the ground and a pleasure to walk along.

The **road** (concrete factory on left) hardly bothers us as, ten metres further on to the right, our path continues on down into the eroded valley (red dot). The typical black

Pírgos – Vothónas – Kamári 27

Santoríni surface ② accompanies us until we have left the vineyards and enter the pumice gorge. Prickly pears stand on the wayside of the deepening eroded valley. For centuries the winter rains have been filing away at the pumice deposits, which are up to 60 m thick.

0.25 The outskirts of **Vothónas** lie in a valley and have a rather pitiful and dilapidated appearance. Many of the typical cave dwellings are still in ruins after the earthquake of 1956, when some 3000 houses were destroyed on the island. The caves are ideal for their inhabitants – cool in the summer and warm in the winter, though unfortunately not very stable.

> *Alternative: In the next valley up on the left, only eight minutes away, is the cave church Panagiatis Sergeinas with a small bell-cote, a (locked) room to celebrate and a cistern ③.*
>
> *The upper part of church consists of a large chamber hewn into the rock, which acted as a hideout during pirate raids in the Middle Ages. Since it is locked, those in-*

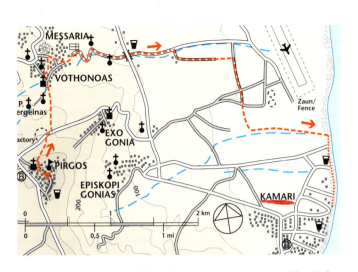

terested should look for the warden in the valley before setting off.

Just before entering the village itself you will come across the large church of Panagía with a huge eucalyptus tree; bear round it and turn left into the small lane. Here you will see a church with six bell-cotes and, further on, a classicistic house. Eventually taking your eyes off this wonderful sight ④, you should return to the valley below the windmill and then head left. The domed church with the nine enormous bell-cotes ⑤ dominates the village from up here. Passing some more cave dwellings ⑥, you go to

0.35 the **end of the village** before leaving the eroded valley via numerous bends. On the right a twin cave church has been dug out of the slope; shortly after, you cross under the **main road** next to a taverna.

Wander along the side road towards the sea for a while,
0.45 then turn off to the right into a lane next to a **group of houses**. Later you will go left, again towards the sea.
0.55 Strolling through vineyards, you come across a **transversal path**, which you should follow to the right, parallel with the airport, dropping down into a hollow. From
1.20 there you can get straight to the black sands of **Kamári** by proceeding along the dry stream-bed. From here it is still another half hour to the bus station!

Pírgos – Vothónas – Kamári 29

❹ Ancient Théra – Never on a Monday!

Along with Akrotíri and Délos, the ancient site of Théra, founded in the 8th century BC, is the main archaeological sight on the Cylcades. This trek leads in four to five hours across the saddle of Mt. Messavounó. Excepting Mondays, when the excavations are closed, you should set off with enough time left to fit in with the opening hours (see below).
■ *8 km, difference in altitude 350 m, moderate*

AWT It is a half-hour bus journey to **Empório:** you should try to sit on the right-hand side of the bus, as the views are often breathtaking.

*The houses of the **kástro**, the old town higher up, are joined together like a castle on the outside and linked by a maze of narrow lanes within. You enter through two covered passages and, with luck, should find your way out again.*

To find where our trek will continue later on, you should first take your bearings on a terrace below the kástro (at the exit marked "1831"). In the fields on the outskirts of the town, at the foot of the mountain to the south-east, is a church with three vaults ②. Approximately 80 m to the right of it is our subsequent route.

After descending the steps from the terrace to the hollow, we bear right, then 200 m down before turning left be-
0.00 tween two barrel-roofed **storehouses** ① on to a narrow dirt track leading up a slight incline. 100 m ahead on the left is the stump of a windmill. The road narrows into a deeply embedded monopáti. On the left in the middle of the fields is the three-vaulted church of Agios Taxiárchis

30 **Santoríni**

②, which we could already see from the kástro above.

0.05 Having turned on to the **dirt track** which comes down from the left, you leave it again at the second right-hand bend, bearing *left* onto a path which runs up to a retaining wall. Going along it, you come to a house with a rural chapel (left). After only a few steps you come across a narrow road, which you should take for 60 m to the left. On the right before a quarry you will see a sunken, well-tend-
0.12 ed monopáti, along which you head on up to a **group of houses** to the right of the track. This becomes a small road and you continue along it, first going left at the fork and then straight on. Brushing past a chapel, you hike left along the foot of the mountain.

Périssa stretches along the coast to the right; the island of Anáfi is visible in the distant background. Planes fly straight towards the rock on which Ancient Théra lies. If you take a closer look, you will discover a small chapel, built daringly into the rock.

0.30 Now we are at the **end of the valley** below; our path uphill ③ lies on the right-hand slope. We keep to the right over the level ground, then cross a monopáti, reaching a metal sign 50 m down the road: now the ascent can begin. The track up to Selláda, as the saddle is known, is fairly steep but can be managed in half an hour. A kantina
1.00 awaits us in the **saddle** above.

> *If you want to visit **Ancient Théra**, you should be there by 2.30 pm, as visitors have to leave the site by 3.00 pm. The site has well-preserved remains of buildings dating from the Egyptian-Ptolemaic era (250 BC) and subsequent Roman times. The excavations were carried out around 1900 by German archaeologists, who also left the*

Empório – Old Théra – Kamári

descriptions. The position of the town and the fact that both the agora and the theatre face the sea are particularly impressive.

Anyone itching to go for a swim can take a minibus from here to the coast. But, never on a Monday.

The route for pleasure-seekers, who should however be fairly steady on their feet, leads to a path heading away from the road to the left at the third right-hand bend. (Otherwise Kamarí can also be reached by staying on the road.)

✓
1.15 The superb hiking trail runs along the mountain high above Kamarí. Later on you come to the chapel of **Zoodóchos Pigí** ("life-giving source") ④ via some steps.

A picture-book site such as can only be found on the Cyclades: in the grotto a masonry table for the visitors to the parish fair and bells hanging in the branches. A heavenly peace reigns up here, only a short way from the hustle and bustle in Kamarí. Even though the life-giving source cannot serve its function, because the cave is barred.

1.30 The road is paved from here, leading down over hairpin bends to the black sands of **Kamarí**.

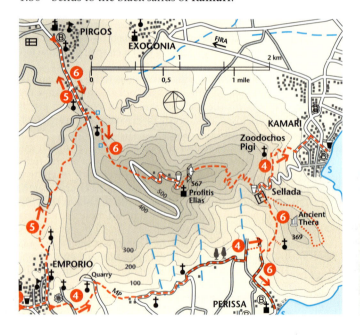

32   Santoríni

⑤ Ascent to Pírgos

This one-and-a-half hour walk can be done almost exclusively on old mule tracks – a rarity on Santoríni. Gentle climbing and two interesting small towns make it a charming outing. The only taverns are to be found in Empório and Pírgos.
■ *4 km, altitude difference 285 m, easy to moderate*

Combining walks 5 and 6 makes it into a three to four-hour, yet difficult tour.

▷ *Map see left*

AWT 0.00 Take the Périssa bus as far as **Empório** and alight at the fork in the road below the large church. Walk down the side road towards the sea, past the school (left), then, when you reach the kindergarten (left) at the road junction, go up to the left. There you will see the tightly grouped houses of the kástros (s. p. 30).

At the next fork, where there is a junction box and a blue sign, bear right towards a gorge. At the end of the village a chapel ① gives us its blessing before we leave the parish just beyond two flying buttresses. A delightful old pathway leads us on down in to a valley. Where it **forks** below a church, we start climbing to the left in zigzags and on up along a ridge ②. Do not be disheartened by the wide

0.15

0.30 **dirt track** to the right, which has to be followed uphill for 100 m, for we soon return to the old mule track on the right. To the left lies Megalochóri and ahead of us the hill village Pírgos. Gradually ascending the slope, we finally

Empório – Pírgos 33

0.45 reach the **road** near the first houses in Pírgos.
> ***Alternative:*** *If you go downhill from here for about 30 m, you will come to a wayside cross and the path up to **Profítis Elías monastery**. Description ⑥.*

Otherwise one stays on the road which, after a dip, leads
0.50 to **Pírgos** bus station.
> *A wander through the narrow streets of this hill village, which was the island's capital during Turkish times, is an absolute must. The Venetians left a kástro here.*

▶ **Bus timetables** may be acquired at the information kiosk in Fíra bus station.

▶ Staying at the caldera: Situated on the promenade of Fíra, north of the boutiques where the traders hang out their wares, is the café "Térpsi". Below it is the small **hotel** "**Katris**", commanding the best views. Tel. 22860 23292.

6 The aerial monastery

The monastery of the prophet Elias has dominated the highest point on Santoríni from time immemorial. The military aerials which have been added in modern times may have disfigured it, but they have also made it unmistakable. The great charm of this three-hour hike lies in the distant views and the almost entirely intact old mule tracks. On top of this come the excavations of Old Théra as a cultural bonus. You will miss tavernas along the way, though. Sporty hikers can start in Empório and follow tour 5 first.
■ *7 km, altitude difference 560 m, moderate to difficult*

▷ Map see page 32

AWT 0.00 — Setting off from **Pírgos** bus station, take the main road in the direction Elias monastery as far as a dip with a right-hand bend, but ignore it. About 150 m further on you will

0.05 — see a **wayside cross** on the left of the road, which has now started to climb. Here a sign marks the old footpath up to the monastery which later passes a tumbledown church ①. Down to the left lies the airport. Following the mountain ridge, walk straight uphill until you reach the

0.25 — **road**. Directly opposite a short path commences, only to terminate at the road again further up. On the road, below the barracks, you should proceed as far as the brick arch-

0.35 — way. Just behind it a footpath leads to them **monastery**, which – surrounded by transmission masts and radar equipment – offers a most curious motif for a photograph.

Pírgos – Profítis Elías – Périssa/Kamári

*The **Profítis Elías monastery** was built between 1711 and 1857. The interlocking complex has no courtyard of any significance. Coming in out of the dazzling light, it takes a while to make out the beautiful fittings in the dark monastery church. The contemplative breather in the cool interior of the church is a godsend.*

0.35 Leaving the **monastery grounds** through a large metal door, we follow the road for a few metres up to the right. About 40 m before the barrier at the entrance to the military camp our path ② veers to the left in a passage through the little wall. Those with a pronounced fear of heights may find the first two hundred metres rather trying. It gets easier after that. Even dwarf pine grows in this windy region and offers at least optical hold. Further down artistically arranged double bends lead us to the car

1.10 park in **Old Théra**.

It lies in the saddle, Greek "selláda", in front of the mountain Messa Voúno. During the summer a kiosk does business here.

It takes ten minutes to reach the tip of the excavated Ptolemaic city, but entrance is only permitted up until 2.30 pm. Read more about the excavations on page 31.

Alternative: if you follow ④ from AWT 1.00, you come to **Kamári**, which has very good bus connections with Fíra.

At the rear of the car park begins a footpath to Périssa. To the right on the mountain stands the whitewashed monastery, beside it the military installation whose garish camouflage stands out over a long distance.

Daring hikers can take a fifteen-minute detour to a chapel in the precipitous rock face by taking a steep path on the left.

Having arrived down on the plain, you should follow the

1.35 roadway to the left in order to reach **Périssa** and the sea, where buses leave for Fíra.

It is also possible to wander along the foot of the mountain for half an hour as far as *Empório* and then catch the same bus from there.

❼ Vineyards

In the south of Santoríni are expansive vineyards which we want to roam through. Using old, sandy mule tracks and dirt tracks we visit the elegant village of Paleochório and later the coast near Akrotíri in two-and-a-half hours. If you are interested, it is wise to enquire about the opening times of the excavation sites there. The route offers places to stop at. To reach the starting point, take the bus either to Athiniós harbour or to Aktrotíri.
■ *6 km, difference in altitude 155 m, easy*

AWT 0.00 Leave the bus at the **crossing** where the roads to the harbour and to Pírgos branch off and walk straight down the road beside the small chapel (right) in the direction "Perissa Beach". Turn off to the right before you come to a long wall, talking a short cut along the wall until you get back
0.05 on to the road. Further down, beyond the **Hotel "Zorbas"**, you go left across the hotel grounds to concrete steps beneath a gap in the wall. Then proceed to the left along the retaining walls. At the end of the vineyard, to the right of some agaves, you descend steeply so as to reach a small eroded valley via a mule track. Follow the depressed path
0.15 and walk on past a **group of houses** with several chapels ① on the left-hand side, partly built in caves. Following a short concrete section the path again becomes rustic.

On the next concrete section, at the sign "Ag. Foterini", go
0.25 uphill to the right and, at the top, left to **Megalochório**. Down in the village, in the beautiful village square in front of the church, is the shady, rather distinguished garden

Megalochório – Akrotíri

tavern "Raki".

From there we continue down the street, disregarding turn-offs to the right. Below the village we rejoin the familiar path, which has unfortunately acquired a concrete cover for quite a long section. Bordered on both sides by walls, it passes through the vineyards. Lying directly on the ground, the roundly bent vines are in a better position to draw the night wetness from the loess soil. This is where the famous "crater wine" originates.

0.45 After passing a cistern (left), cross the **road** to Périssa and continue along the dry streambed, all the time heading towards the sea. Commencing at a con-
0.55 struction storage site, a **dirt track** leads us on past a cistern
1.05 (right) to the chapel **Agía Anna** ②, where we continue straight ahead.

Taking a transversal dirt track for a short distance to the right, we leave it again before it starts to climb and follow a
1.25 wide dry bed down to the **sea**. The scarcely frequented black beach has some areas where the stones are smaller. Keeping to the coast, you come to the road and on up to
1.35 the **excavations of Akrotíri** (s. next page), where there is good bus service to Fíra.

⑧ Akrotíri

After visiting the world-famous Minoan excavations, you climb up to the village of Akrotíri, wandering first along the edge of the crater before reaching a pleasant place to stop, in front of a rock chapel on the flat seaward side of the island. Then it's off for a swim. You can choose between a practically empty and a thoroughly organized beach.
■ *8 km, difference in altitude 230 m, easy to moderate*

AWT Take the bus to the **Akrotíri excavations**. In peak season the archaeological site is open until 7.00 pm, so you could also visit it after the trek.

The excavations of Akrotíri are one of the greatest archaeological sensations of the last century. The uncovered parts are 3500 years old and the two layers underneath are said to be as much as 8000 years old. A free plan is available at the ticket office. Important sites are supplied with descriptions and reproductions of the frescoes found there. The plaster cast of the famous wooden bed is exhibited at the end of the tour. The bed burned during the hot rain of pumice stone and was only preserved as an imprint. The measurements give an approximate idea of the size of the people of the period.

0.00 The trek begins at the **memorial** above the car park. From here, a path leads left to a terrace. You go along the retaining wall until you cross a monopáti, which meanders along the foot of the slope. Going right, you walk across the floor of a valley ① up to a road, turn right here to the main road and then up left to the bus stop in

Akrotíri – Panagía Kinísi – Red Beach – Akrotíri   39

0.15 **Akrotíri**. Bearing left uphill from the bus stop to the neoclassical school, you continue in the direction of the beak of the eagle seated on the monument. Anyone wanting to have a quick look at the narrow streets of the kástro should take the steps on the left.

From these steps you go round the church to the right and head up to the road. You remain on it until you reach the hairpin bend, where a lane leads you on uphill to the
0.20 left. Take the first lane on the left, going past a **lowered chapel** and a tight cluster of houses. At the end of the village is another chapel on the left. Here you go right along the concrete road up to a fork (minimarket on right), and then left. Continuing on through the next group of houses, you turn right on to a narrow concrete track which is lined by stone walls on both sides and come past an out-
0.25 standing new **villa** ②. At the next bend we have the magnificent panorama of the "inland sea" with the three
★ towns Oía, Fíra and mountainside Pírgos, above which – as on every Cycladic island – Prophet Elias keeps watch from his mountain top.

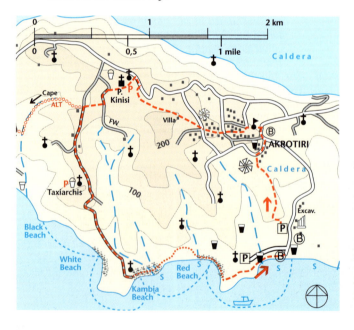

40   Santoríni

The mule track leads us further, almost without any effort on our part, to a road which we follow for 50 m to a twin chapel. There is a sign leading down a stepped path to
0.35 **Panagía Kinísi** ③ (P: N 36°21.697'/ E 25°23.196', 145 m). Ahead of the paled gate of this pilgrimage church we bear left on to the mule track ④ towards the lighthouse on Cape Akrotíri. Below the mountain peak to the southwest is a chapel – later our resting spot!

You wander on over the flat, between the vines growing on the ground. Perhaps we should try some of the island wine this evening! It thrives here because the volcanic rock is particularly fertile and the pumice absorbs the dew, then releases it gradually. The grape harvest takes place as early as the end of August.

A dirt track crosses ahead and you follow it left for 80 m. At the left bend, bear right on to a hewn path. Then go
0.40 left on the next **dirt track**.

Alternative: if you want to wander on to Cape Akrotíri, you have to climb down into the small eroded valley

Akrotíri – Panagía Kinísi – Red Beach – Akrotíri   41

straight ahead. Turning right ahead of a solitary tree, you follow some charming paths above the sea and reach the wonderfully old-fashioned lighthouse in 50 minutes.

Our main route leads towards the chapel on the rock. The dirt road offers little for the eye – just ordinary country-side. Yet soon we come out of our visual depression: we

0.50 walk up a few metres to the **taxiarchis** (archangel) **chapel** ⑤ (**P:** N 36°21.290'/ E 25°23.909', 105 m) and do something here for our spiritual welfare, for our eyes and against our thirst. Besides blessing every drop of water from the cistern, Saint Paraskeví also restores poor eye-sight. Below the resting spot a wide landscape, in which several half-finished buildings have accumulated, opens up before us. A shady bench has been built for our siesta... We speed on downhill over the dirt road towards the sea

1.10 and the little frequented white sands of "**Kambia Beach**" with cantina. Anyone looking for a more lively beach

1.20 should walk on over the cliffs to "**Red Beach**" ⑥. Despite the numerous sun-shades and sunbeds, it offers little in the way of catering. In the summer kaikis are available to take you further or to "Black Beach".

Over the red cliffs and then along the sea with good taver-

1.35 nas you arrive back at the **bus stop**.

Museum of Cycladic Art in Athens

Starting from Syntagma Square, it is a five-minute walk along Vasilissis Sofias Street to the Museum of *Cycladic & Ancient Greek Art* in Neofitou Douka St. 4.

This private museum has the most comprehensive collection of Cycladic idols on an area of 2,000 m2.

On display here are about 350 exhibits from what is the oldest civilization in Europe as well as finds from the Neolithic and Hellenistic Ages. A visit to this museum is the perfect way to round off a trip to the Cyclades.

Open from 10 am to 4 pm, Saturdays until 3 pm, *closed Tuesdays and Sundays.*

42   Santoríni

9 A day on Thirassía

Santoríni's sister island – Thirassía – forms the western edge of the island which had been perfectly circular up until the eruption of 1600 BC.
A small boat sails from Santoríni's harbour Amoúdi, below Oía, several times a day. As it only takes up to four hours to explore the isle on foot, it is possible to return in the evening. It is advisable to sail across to Ríva/Agía Eríni in the morning and to remember to ask when a boat will be returning from Kórfos, the other harbour, in the evening.
If a shorter stay is preferred, a two-hour walk is also possible.
■ *7 km, difference in altitude 240 m, moderate*

AWT To the north of **Ríva** stands the chapel of Agía (Ital. "Santa") Eríni, from which the name *Santoríni* originated in
0.00 Venetian times. Starting at the boat, bear left along the harbour and up to the right in front of Cpt. Micháli's har-
0.05 bour tavern. Shortly afterwards you pass a **chapel** 1 and continue inland after a right and then a left turn. Ignore
0.10 the **turn-off** on a concrete road leading up to the left and instead walk straight ahead on a dirt track. A remarkable number of mules can still be seen on the thinly populated island. Soon a group of inter-connected chapels comes into view and, right above them on the horizon, a triple chapel – our first destination! Before you know it, you
0.25 reach the first **chapel** Marinou Sirigou, then you stay on a
0.30 **road** for 80 m.

Short cut: Some experience in path-finding is required

Thirassía – Ríva – Manólas   43

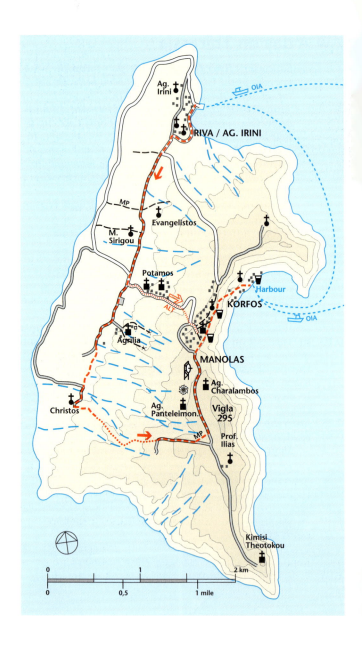

for the tour described below. Those who do not have any experience take the left fork on this road up to Manólas in 20 minutes, passing the many churches in Potamós ② village.

0.35 Those who wish to do the full tour walk straight on until they pass the large **Agrilia** church standing on the left in an eroded valley. It is surrounded by the ruins caused by the 1956 earthquake. Continue horizontally, turning left at the fork after 50 m, following a mule track for a while
0.50 and finally a country lane which leads to the **Christos Chapel** ③: a place to rest and drink water.

The ascent begins opposite the small door on a wide path which, however, peters out further up, making it necessary to work one's way up from terrace to terrace without any paths. Two churches are visible yonder on the mountain, but with a valley in-between. Proceed on up the middle of the ridge, before heading for the small summit chapel Profítis Elías. On the upper reaches of the slope it is possible to use a track again. On the right appears the abandoned monastery Kimísi (Ascension), which dominates the tip of the island like a lighthouse.

1.20 Higher up a monopáti branches off to the left and leads us
1.30 to a transversal **road** beneath the Elias chapel. Heading
1.40 left, it passes the **Panteleimonas Church** (left) and on down to **Manólas**.

★ You have a choice of places to rest: a magnificent view from the top of the village ④ or the maritime atmosphere
1.55 down in **Kórfos harbour**, from where the boat returns.

Thirassía – Ríva – Manólas 45

Sífnos

Two mountain ranges of white marble run through the fertile green island. The lower-lying areas mainly consist of mica schist, a sandy sedimentary rock raised from the sea. The lush vegetation with numerous olive groves and the many gently sloping mule tracks still in use make Sífnos one of the most popular islands for Cycladic walkers.

Apollonía, the high-lying little capital town, is the best place from which to set off on walks; thanks to their good bus connections, though, Kamáres and Platís Gialós can also be recommended. Sífnos is one of the islands which are easy to reach for Athenians with the new fast ships. Places to stay can therefore become rather overcrowded on summer weekends.

The trails through the delightful landscape pass countless monasteries, many chapels and even wells. In addition the villages, each with their own characteristics, provide worthwhile destinations for the walker. And good bus connections guarantee a safe return from every trek.

Accurate maps by John Birkett-Smith (1995, 1:40,000) and from the Greek publishers Anavasi (2002, 1:25,000) are available in the shops. The former shows almost all the mule tracks, but hardly any dirt tracks or roads, while the latter does not show all the monopátia. So it is best to have both. Particularly recommended are hikes 10, 16, 20 and 21 as described in the book.

⑩ The Way to Saint Lazarus

Those who can spare three-and-a-half hours will experience one of the most beautiful walks on the Cyclades. Using wall-lined mule tracks, we explore the picture-book Greek landscape around Apollonía. In the middle section a couple of places are sometimes overgrown – which is why long trousers are an advantage. A good cistern awaits us at the half-way point.

■ *8 km, difference in altitude 75 m, moderate*

AWT 0.00 — A stair-path leads up to Artemónas from beside the old-fashioned "Café Lakis" on **memorial square** in **Apollonía** (175 m). Up on the right is the large domed church,

0.10 — from where the path leads to a hollow with a **bridge**. (Picnic items can be purchased in the supermarket to the right of the bridge). The steps of the skála lead uphill again to the elongated square in **Artemónas**. To the left of the shady ouzerie "Margerita" the lane continues straight on for about 150 m through fashionable Artemónas with its attractive gardens and manor-houses.

You go left at a house blocking the way. On the right after

0.15 — 100 m is a **church** directly on the lane and, a little further on the left-hand side, the large church of Kóchi with its blue dome. You have to go down the gentle incline immediately on your left and then second right. Mt. Profitis Elias lies above to the left and the antennae to the right as you leave the houses behind you. Some 350 m after the

0.20 — church of Kóchi you reach the **end of the village**.

Veer right at a sharp fork. On the right is a metal signpost

48   Sífnos

which we follow for a while: Agios Symeon! With each step the path mainfestly becomes a dream monopáti, cut deeply into the hillside in parts like the lanes leading to the cellars in Austrian wine-growing villages – only here they are lined with olive trees ①. It's more strolling than hiking. After a well (left) it becomes rocky underfoot for a while until we reach a dirt track, where we must not forget to take the right-angled **left turn**. The metal sign is 10 m after the fork.

0.30

Head for the two summit churches on the horizon, then go down and turn left at a fork. On the right in the middle of the fields is the Dimitri Chapel ② with a cistern. After a **hollow** the mule track meanders idyllically along the slope, we bear towards the summit chapel of Agios Lazaros and finally drop down slightly to the large **drinking-fountain** ③ hewn into the rock to the right of the path (**P:** N 36°59.696'/ E 24°42.467').

★

0.40

0.50

From there you walk to the bottom of the valley and now leave the marked route to Simon's monastery *to the left* and head down the valley for 20 m. On the right you will find a quiet **stair-path** which leads up the terraced slope. At the top on the left stands the summit chapel of Saint Lazarus with a cistern (235 m). Although closed, it makes a magnificent place to rest and enjoy the view.

!!

1.00

A few houses have been put in its care. Here the dirt track passes two rectangular **stone towers** which taper towards the top.

1.05

> *The towers are the summit station of the former material cableway of the Voríni iron ore mine, now a refuse dump, further up the hill. Iron ore was extracted there from the end of the 19th century until the 1920s, when it became*

unprofitable. The ore was transported from here to the valley. Along the route of the present-day dirt track ran a railway which also served to haul the ore (s. p. 52).

If you wish to shorten the walk described below, you should follow this dirt track as far as Kamáres (AWT 2.55). Although the last section has been asphalted, you are rewarded with splendid views of the sea.

Friends of the Greek monopáti hence proceed downhill

1.05 for some meters on a dirt track to the left of the **towers** until they reach a metal gate, to the right of which they discover an old mule track. Although seldom used and therefore somewhat overgrown in its upper reaches, it is still passable.

It passes through pleasant, pastoral landscape with terraced olive groves. At a sort of "crossing" (on the left the entrance to an olive grove) our route continues straight on downhill. Then the monopáti veers horizontally to the left. Later there is a fence on the right, followed by a bend. After a right turn-off, which we ignore, and a left-

1.30 hand bend we find ourselves standing **above the upper retaining dam**. Following a short descent we reach the

1.35 **side valley of the Kamáres**, where ① turns off to the right for Kamáres.

If we look to the left, we see the stone pyramids neatly piled up on the rocks and the no less artistic flight of steps hewn into the rock mass. Now comes a five-minute as-

1.40 cent, but this is mitigated by a first **view of Apollonía** from up above.

Five minutes beyond the Panagía chapel on the right we come to a crossing, where we proceed straight on, neither up nor down. Later the path starts to climb a little. At a

1.55 **fork**, above which on the left stands a chapel, we turn left. Following a short ascent we are greeted at the top by a vaulted chapel (right) ④.

Very soon we are surrounded by houses, after which we

2.05 go left up the **concrete/sand road** and then, before reaching the hump, right on to a monpáti at the power pole. After a chapel (right) we reach the *skála*, the stair-

2.15 path down to the main square in **Apollonía**.

50 **Sífnos**

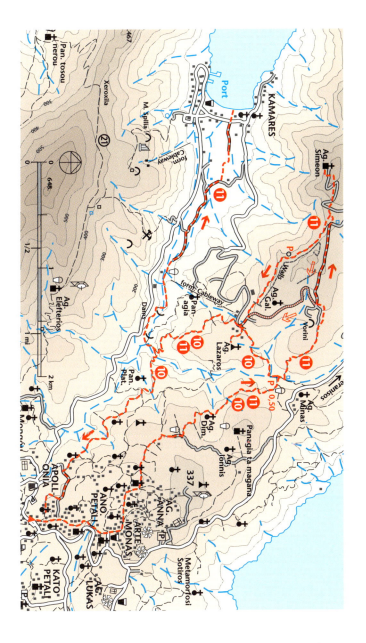

Apollonía – Artemónas – Agios Lazaros – Apollonía 51

⓫ The Way to Saint Simon

A trek of four to five hours through fields and valleys to the monastery of Agios Símeon, high above the bay of Kamarí. Easily identifiable paths offer fantastic views across the whole of Sífnos. Opportunities for bathing and eating abound at the end of the tour in Kamarí.

■ *12 km, difference in altitude 430 m, difficult*

▷ *Map see previous page*

AWT 0.50

★

Start by following **walk** 10 as far as AWT 0.50; map page 51. From the **well** (**P:** N 36°59.696'/ E 24°42.467) you go down a few metres into the dry bed, bearing right after 100 m to another modern cistern before climbing up a splendid stair-path ①.

Unfortunately, the attractive steps turn into a scree path further up, but we have come a good bit closer to our destination, Mt. Simon. To the left of the path you will see

1.10 (and smell) the former iron ore mine of **Voríni**, which is now filled in with rubbish.

This is one of the five ancient mines on Sífnos. The iron ore found here contains a lot of silver. In the 5th century BC slaves lying prostrate in their shackles drove the narrow tunnels into the mountainside, advancing 30 cm a day. The silver was minted in Aegina, making Sífnos the wealthiest Aegean island in antiquity. Lead was also produced from the silver mining. Iron ore working was recommenced in 1900 and continued into the 1920s.

Beside the mine turn right on the dirt track and walk on

1.20 until you approach a **water tank** on the left-hand side. 30 m ahead of it turn left on to an old pilgrims' path, which you now use alternately with the track leading up to the
1.35 **summit monastery of Agios Símeon** (480 m).

It lies far removed, above the sea. As soon as you enter the courtyard, the view pans out across the entire grounds on to the open, glittering sea ②. *A place of absolute tranquillity. The windows allow a glimpse of the church and the long tables used to host the pilgrims. Sitting on the monastery wall, one can look straight down into the fjord of Kamarí, our destination. Time for a summit drink, if needs be from the faucet in the monastery courtyard. Further west is another monastery on a steep mountain: Prof. Elias II, which would take another 20 minutes to reach. Far out to sea further Cycladic islands await us: Mílos with Kímolos and Sérifos.*

1.35 The first stretch back from the **monastery** is the same as the way up. Shortly after crossing the dirt track for the
1.45 second time at the hairpin bend, you should turn off **to the right** away from the well maintained part of the paved path, about 100 m above the walled-in goat pen. The path continues below the walls running towards us on the slope ③.

Alternative: Those who suffer from *severe* vertigo should also use the already familiar track for the return leg, turning off to the right before the refuse mine and returning to the track again after 20 minutes at the two stone towers (AWT 2.10).

Proceed along the clearly visible path marked with colour dots, past the pen (left), later keeping at a distance of 40 m below the dry walls. First you come to a broader path

Apollonía – Agios Symeon – Kamáres 53

which then becomes a hiking trail leading through elder bushes. The Kamáres valley is on the right, sometimes steeply right below the path.

The route flattens out whenever you reach the remains of a round lime kiln (P: N 36°59.833'/ E 24°41.662'). (You should not follow the blue arrow about 20 m above it, nor should you go through the gap in the wall!). Now the path slowly descends, always in close proximity to the wall on the left. Apollonía has come into view on the horizon and in the foreground, right beside the dirt track, are two massive towers which taper towards the top – our half-way point. Up to the left stands the summit church of Agios Lazaros.

Having gone through a small door, you soon come to a dirt track to the left above the path; go down to the right from there ④. You then descend immediately to the left of

2.10 the **stone towers**, the summit station of a former material cableway (s. p. 49).

2.35 Follow the description of **walk 10** as far as the **side valley** (there from AWT 1.05 to 1.35). Walk 10 then leads up to the left to Apollonía.

We go to the right into the main valley and up to the dirt track on the other side, which brings us to the lower (larger) dam. Down in the stream-bed it is possible to assess the structural damage to the newly constructed dam. It is ready to be blown up, without ever having been put into operation...

Once in the dry stream-bed, walk on down for 200 m until you see on the right a water tank with a faucet. This is where the former cableway ended.

Go left along the proper dirt road which begins near a group of houses, moving right at the first fork to another dirt track which runs one metre higher up. Go left at the next fork and shortly afterwards on to a monpáti, which

3.05 finishes at a dirt track leading to **Kamáres**.

▶ Taxi tel.: 22840-31925   6932 403 485

⑫ Above the Sea

This three-hour tour with great views starts from Kástro, first along the coast, then on raised ground above the sea. It mostly leads along old paths and hence away from any tavernas. By walking through a green valley, you come to Apollonía via Artemónas.

■ *8 km, difference in altitude 250 m, moderate*

AWT 0.00 From the isthmus outside **Kástro** you wander below the **windmills**, at first on a road along the coast. After 120 m, opposite the power pole with a direction sign (right), you find a glorious path on the left which, later briefly interrupted by a dirt track, meanders between two narrow walls half way up the terraces above the sea ①. Contentedly, you arrive first at a chapel and then at **Panagía Poulátí**. Below the church, directly on the path, you may like to enjoy a Cycladic resting spot in a small, walled garden ... gentle terraces which you never tire of seeing lie between here and Kástro.

★ 0.20

In severe heat it is worth taking three minutes to nip down to the spring by the rocky shore.

Ahead of the car park begins an ascending kalderími. The picturesque old stair-path ② is thrice severed by the rough dirt track. You can use the windmill of Agios Loúkas as a bearing. Cross the **road** at the small holiday houses. The path takes you past the restored windmill (right) of Agios Loúkas and ends in front of a stockyard up on the level ground. Bearing right here, you soon see a wonderfully situated **cemetery** on the right. Continue straight ahead

0.35

0.40

Kástro – Ag. Loúkas – Ag. Anna – Artemónas – Apollonía 55

on the road in a northerly direction and left at a junction. Below the village of Artemónas (with two windmills) you !! turn *right* after a left-hand bend in the road (on the right are two elongated holiday houses) on to a wall-lined track. Soon afterwards this is interrupted by a dirt track, which you cross. To the left of a new building you discover a path sloping gently up to the road (P: N 36°59.162' / E 24°43.566'). On the other side is a dirt track which leads
0.50 to the old flagstone path up to **Agía Anna**.

Short cut: by going left along the valley in Agía Anna, you can reach Apollonía in 25 minutes via Artemónas. The next stretch of the way leads up to the right between the houses. The hill with the aerial masts, at the foot of
0.55 which is a **cemetery**, rises up to the left. A short distance later you turn off the dirt track to the right. This is where a wonderful, peaceful panoramic way heads north, high above the sea, following the contour lines. Antíparos and Páros lie on the horizon. The demarcation formed by the wall on the left-hand side of the path is missing for a while. Where the wall reappears further on, a steel water pipe has been laid. Finally the path veers left, heading in-
1.05 land, towards a **dirt track**.

Turning left in a southerly direction, you find yourself on a plateau with the Panagía ta Magána monastery to the right on the opposite slope. Once again, who other than Prophet Elias keeps watch over it all! On our way between
1.15 the field walls we come past a **St. John's chapel** 3, then proceed straight ahead. The walls are getting higher here
1.20 and, at a **fork** (metal sign to Símeon Monastery in the opposite direction), we go left.

Between the walls 4 appears Artemónas. But before

56 Sífnos

      reaching it, you come to two major forks along the way: at the first you go down to the right and at the second up to the left. Now you only have to resist the temptation posed by the two shady tavernas on the oblong square
1.30 in **Artemónas**, in order to get safely back down to
1.40 **Apollonía** via the steps of the splendid skála.

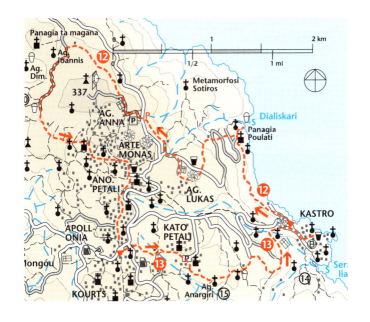

⑬ From Apollonía to Kástro

This tour of 1½ hours leads through varied, agricultural landscape on the eastern side of the island, heading along solitary Cycladic trails to Kástro, the former capital, where it is possible to join walk 12.
■ *3 km, difference in altitude 180 m, easy*

▷ *Map see previous page*

AWT To the left of the raised site with the war memorial on the
0.00 **platía in Apollonía** a lane leads into the maze of houses. We follow it for 50 m to a stair-path which leads down to the left, pass beneath the road and then go immediately down to the right. Soon coming into view on the hill opposite is the wonderful paved track to the village of **Káto Petáli** ①. Having come through the valley dotted with olive trees and over a bridge, you reach the village and
0.10 pass to the right of it. At the other end is a **large church** with a blue dome. Descending a few steps to the right, you go across the car park and head along a narrow concrete path on the other side to a sort of suburb.

Here you proceed down a slight incline and then – opposite a chapel on the other side of the valley ② – left above the valley. After having passed a dovecote tower (right), you bear left (red dot) at a fork up on to a beautiful winding Cycladic trail.

0.15 Soon you see the **twin chapel Anargýri** ③ between the trees on the right, where you turn off left again. Then come two forks within 10 m of each other: bear left at the first and right at the second! The xirolithíes on either side

58   Sífnos

0.20 are quite enormous. 50 m beyond a flat-roofed **chapel** (right) you turn off right and again in front of a garden belonging to a house.

After touching a concrete path leading down to the left, you continue straight ahead along a monopáti towards a
0.25 hill. Before the **hilltop** the path veers to the right, loses height, is then interrupted for a few metres and finally crosses another mule track. That is where you turn off left, walking downhill with a splendid view of Kástro 4. Down below runs a dirt track, which you follow for 50 m to the left, when you find another monopáti on the right. Passing above the cemetery, this brings you down to the eroded rocks in the valley and up to the road and the windmills. The lane leading up to the bus turning place in
0.45 **Kástro** starts there.

If you prefer to take a dip first, walk on until you reach Serália, Kástro's harbour, with a tiny beach and a taverna.

Kástro is Sífnos' medieval first town. The abutting houses are built so as to form a fortress on the exterior, curving around the centre with its narrow lanes and churches, by way of protection. The very old settlement also possesses the ruins of an acropolis dating back to antiquity. The finds which have been made there are on display in the local archaeological museum.

⑭ From Fáros to Kástro

This two-hour tour can be used to prolong walks 15 and 16. It is also recommended in its own right, though – above all on account of the surprising vista it affords of Kástro.
■ *4.5 km, difference in altitude 140 m, easy*

AWT 0.00 — In **Fáros** you ascend the step-path in the higher western part, passing the Nicholas chapel at the end of the village. The wide paved path leads up through treeless fields on

0.15 — terraces. Follow the **dirt track** which then comes uphill for about 30 m, until you rediscover the already familiar monopáti, which later takes you past the solar installa-

0.25 — tion (right) to the **road**.
Go up the road to the left for 120 m, turning off on to a monopáti on the right 20 m beyond a water reservoir.
After eight minutes the monopáti divides on an expansive area with a cattle-trough (**P:** N 36°57.519'/ E 24°44.733). Climb up to the left there, taking the path to the right after 50 m. Further on you find another cattle-trough, where you go right across the valley bottom, then left up the hill

0.45 — to the small **country chapel** ①.
Stroll on between high walls leading through olive groves, turn right towards the sea, then up to the left at the next fork and after that straight ahead until you catch

0.55 ★ — **sight of Kástro** ② at the end of the defile. Out to sea lie Antíparos and Páros. The path first brings you down to

1.15 — the small bathing place of Serália and then to **Kástro**. After walking round the pretty town (see p.59) you still have time for refreshments before the bus comes.

60 Sífnos

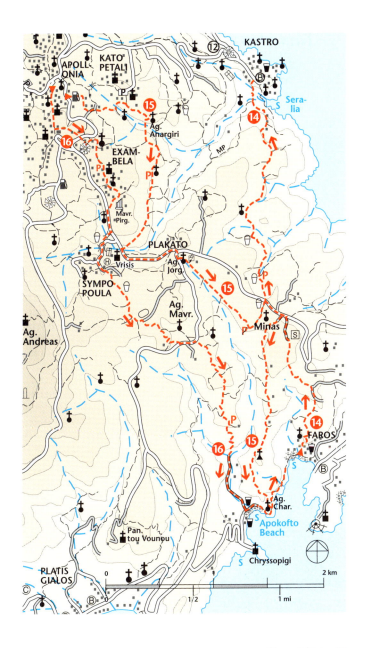

Fáros – Kástro 61

⑮ Moní Vrísis

This three-hour tour leads through terraced agricultural land from Apollonía to Fáros. Apart from one short section of road the walk only follows old mule tracks, which is what makes it such an experience. Along the way we pass the large fortified monastery of Vrísis, the only one that is still inhabited and open in the mornings. Its romantic inner courtyard is an ideal place to relax.

■ *7 km, difference in altitude 180 m, moderate*

▷ Map see previous page

AWT 0.00	Immediately to the left of a **petrol station** on the eastern edge of **Apollonía**, on the road to Fáros, you go down a narrow ramp. After 15 m turn on to the concrete path on the right and, after another 100 m, bear left up old steps. At a house on the left at a bend, proceed until you come to a transverse lane at a shed. Here you first turn downhill to the left and then, 30 m further between two houses, hori-
0.05	zontally to the **right**. The annoying concrete surface soon ends, the route reverting to a proper path between high dry-stone walls; later it goes down ① in the direction of Ká-
0.10	to Petáli. Turn left at a fork, traverse the **dry bed** and head up to the houses, but do *not* go left into the village.
0.15	At the edge of the valley, whose right-hand side is marked by a beautiful chapel, we pass a dovecote (right), go uphill at a **fork** and then come to a fork where the barrel-vaulted chapel of **Anargýri** (p. 59 ③) with two transepts stands down to the right. It is dedicated to the medical saints

62 Sífnos

Kosmas and Damian, who took no silver (anargýri) in return for the treatment they gave.

Here you drop down to the right, leaving the chapel with the memorial slab in front on your left. On the other side of the following tropically proliferating valley you climb

0.20 up and, when you reach a **fork**, walk to the left along the contour lines. Spread out on the left is a classic Greek terrace landscape, criss-crossed by old country paths. Turn right uphill at the next fork (only half of Kástro can be seen from this vantage point). Dream on through the cornfields with olive trees until you come to a flat-roofed

0.25 **chapel** (left) ② (**P:** N 36°57.999'/ E 24°44.070'). From the forecourt you can see cars driving past further up.

If you follow the path, you reach a fork with signposts. (Down to the left is the direct way to Kástro. The paths heading in our direction are no longer passable.)

We go *right* uphill here, still only taking notice of the landscape and not of the turn-offs on either side, and turn up to the right again at a sharp-cornered fork. All of a sudden,

0.35 after a **bend**, we behold the massive fortified monastery of Vrísis ahead of us ③, while Agios Andreas greets us from above. We are soon at the road, where we go left for a bit

0.40 and then up the well-worn steps to **Panagía Vrísis monastery**.

> *The son who came from a very short relationship between a nun and a sailor founded this fortified monastery, which is only inhabited by two monks now, in 1654. If you proceed beneath the cell block you come out in to the picturesque inner courtyard dominated in the middle by a cruciform domed basilica with valuable fittings.*

0.50 Take the road for another 300 m as far as a **road junction** at the hamlet Plakáto and go right there for about 20 m – direction Chrissopigí. At the house standing in front of a church you walk left down on to a footpath and immediately feel the better for it. Yet from time to time your enthusiasm may also be dampened: occasionally oil can be seen seeping down the mule track from the electricity station up to the left.

A little further down you veer left and stay above the valley. The walls are now lower, thus permitting you to enjoy the countryside all around. Keep your direction at a fork, in other words do not go down to the right. There now follows a section of the route which tends to be overgrown at three or four places. After that our path branches

1.05 up to the left in front of a **garden gate** (**P:** N 36°57.274'/ E 24°44.650')

The path leading uphill starts off narrow and overgrown, later a chapel is visible some way off on a hill to the right and behind it, on the peninsula, the Chrissopigí chapel. The path divides. (On the right is a path leading to the Mínas chapel, from where one could take a short cut by walking next to an overgrown mule track.)

1.10 It is simpler to go left to the road, beside which is a **water tank** where the locals like to draw their water. From there you march about 100 m down the road and turn off in to the *first* dirt track on the right. It is lined by walls and leads to a crossing, where you go straight on towards the sea, past two small water basins (left). Our destination is the hilltop chapel ④.

1.25 The path drops, goes through a **gateway** and shortly afterwards, at a place surrounded by walls, up to the *left*. We pass some distance to the right of the hilltop chapel, sub-

1.40 sequently walking down to the **Charalambos chapel**. But first we sit down on the rocks to delight in the panorama across the Chrissopigí peninsula. The sort of spot dreams are made of.

1.50 It is only a few more steps to the left along the sea to **Fáros**. From there one could join walk 14 to Kástro or, lazy as we are, just wait for the bus.

⑯ The Most Scenic Spot

An easy trek of three-and-a-half hours from Apollonía to the church of Chryssopigí, "the" most scenic spot on the island. The well-defined tracks lead gently downhill all the way to the seaside with its attractive tavernas and a bathing beach!
■ *6.5 km, difference in altitude 230 m, moderate*

▷ Map see page 61

AWT 0.00	From between the cake-shop and the map of the island on the **main square of Apollonía** you walk 40 m to the main alley "Odos Prodou", which leads up to the right.
0.05	*30 m ahead of the large domed church, on the right, is the flat-roofed church of **Agios Sóstis** (1768) with a picturesque forecourt and a series of ancient frescoes along the walls inside.*

Level with the steps on the left is a high wall belonging to the grammar school. Before this we turn left on to the narrow path – first walking downhill, then to the right, where it is somewhat overgrown, up to the road. On the other side we continue between windmill ruins and, immediately afterwards, to the left. Skirting the left-hand,

0.15 seaside edge of **Exámbela**, you pass a shady **chapel** ①
0.20 and, depending on your ability, you arrive more or less speedily at the **blue domed church** of St. Nicholas (**P:** N 36°57.997/ E 24°43.752,230 m), where you enter an alley on the left. Our way leads down right at the fork in front of a row of houses and then left again five metres further on. This track, which soon starts to decline, first heads

Apollonía – Exámbela – Chryssopigí – Fáros

towards the sea, then right and later past the remains of an ancient circular tower standing in a farm to the left of the track. The impressive ruin, the "Mavros Pirgos" (black tower), was built in the 3rd to 6th century BC without mortar using precisely hewn stones. Some 55 of these tower bases still exist on the island; they served as places of refuge and for transmitting light signals. Further downhill you come to the road, which you follow down to the left for about 220 m before leaving it again to the right (200 m further on stands the large Vrísis monastery, see p. 63).

0.30 **Steps** lead down from the road to a monopáti and two bridges in the valley. At a washing place you come to a concrete track. We follow this up right. Above us on the left is the cemetery chapel. When the concrete track forks,

0.35 you head left up to the **helicopter landing pad**.
40 m beyond that you make your way right into the realm of the monopátia and towards the sea. Another tower keeps watch on a hill to the left and the vast St. Andrew's monastery resides above to the right. High walls on the right-hand side of the path guide us reliably ahead. We stroll on over pleasant paving stones, past a cistern with a

0.40 nice place to sit. Heading down left at a **fork**, you do *not* head for the football ground at the second turn-off you come to, but *right* towards the sea (blue dots). The church of Mavroundi ② then appears in a hollow on the left; we stay right at the fork ahead of it. Far below, the day's goal is already discernible: the church of Chryssopigí on the rocky peninsula.

0.50 After crossing the **road** on a slant to the left, you wander up the trail to the *left of a dirt track*. Disregard right-angled turn-offs on either side. Go straight ahead before a *high wall*, then *down to the right* before a wall at a fork (**P:** N 36°57.024'/ E 24°44.514'). The going becomes rather

1.15 steep down to a dry stream-bed, from where a **sandy path** leads you out of the gorge to the shore. We have reached our destination.

1.20 *Chryssopigí church (p. 46), which dates from 1650, lies on a peninsula and possesses a miraculous icon. Children are baptized outside on the rocky promontory, directly above the sea. A "place of strength".*

If you're not keen to swim or sit and relax under the tamarisks of a taverna, stroll on along the wonderful

1.35 coastal path, past a chapel, to **Fáros**.

⑰ Juniper

The south-western part of Sífnos is covered with juniper bushes which lend the region a Nordic touch. This lonely countryside between Platís Gialós and Vathí is criss-crossed by narrow paths which make it a wonderful area in which to hike.
If you only do the first and most interesting part of the route as far as Fikiáda bay and then turn back, it will take three to four hours, whereas the whole tour takes about six. There are neither wells nor tavernas along the entire route.
■ *9/11.5 km, differences in altitude 100/230 m, moderate/difficult*

AWT From the *last* **bus station in Platís Gialós** you go 150 m
0.00 in the direction of Lazárou and just beyond a power pole turn right on to a flat dust road which starts off straight
0.05 and then veers to the left. At the **fork** you walk up to the left. Beyond a left-hand bend you see Lazárou bay down to the left. After coming back it is possible to relax there on the small beach of a delightful inn.
0.10 At the **end of the dust road** begins a narrow path which meanders along above the coastline through rocks and
0.30 juniper bushes. A small **clearing** has formed on raised ground (**P:** N 36°55.266′/ E 24°43.432′).

After that you look down on the next bay and the offshore island of Kitrianí ①. The juniper bushes lend the landscape a very green, totally "non-Greek" appearance. Kímolos and the chalk coastline of Mílos create a frame in the background. Later the path runs by the sea, which has

Plátis Gialós – Fikiáda – Profítis Elías – Plátis Gialós   67

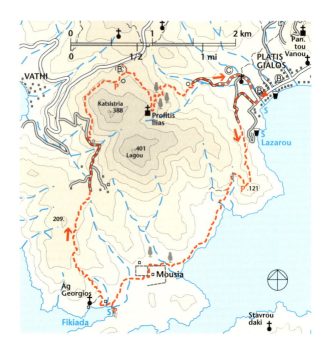

          moulded the rocks into bizarre shapes. Then it leads
0.50 through a **gateway**, turns further inland at a "fork" and starts to climb slightly.

On the left you see a large, two-storey house which can be approached through a gap in the wall. Its name is
1.05 "Mousía". 15 m to the right of the **house** is an opening in the wall, behind which you should immediately turn right. After a further opening, bearing slightly to the left between old olive trees, you continue along a clearly
1.15 visible goat path to **Fikiáda beach** (**P:** N 36°54.421'/ E 24°42.360'). The fine sand is ideal for relaxation. A chapel makes the experience truly Greek.

It is possible to turn back here.

The wall which leads away from the beach has an opening after 30 m, after which you go left and above the coastline, later on steps, to the next, smaller bay with a goat pen.

15 m inland, behind a ruin, starts an ascending path, be-

68   **Sífnos**

low which you later see the chapel on the left and from the top of which you have a fine view of the sea. Directly beneath you lies the southernmost point of Sífnos. 145 m above the sea you first continue inland horizontally. With a flatter mountain ridge to your left you head towards the high table-top mountain Lagou.

1.50   Below some farmhouses you come across strange grey piles of sand and further to the left a **dirt track**. While this later offers a distant view over Vathí bay, it is otherwise rather tedious.

2.00   After the **gully** which runs down from the double mountain on the right you walk up as far as the next bend, where the mountain peters out. There on the right you see a few ruins, among them an ancient watchtower. 50 m beyond that you turn off to the right at an acute angle – in other words in the opposite direction – and come to a new metal gate.

2.05   Directly opposite you discover the **beginning of the path** which will lead you round Mount Katsístria. Climbing strenuously, the sight of the swimming pool in Vathí may make you think of doing better things than plodding along at an altitude of 230 m. But such thoughts will not help you now.

2.25   The path passes a round **goat pen** (P: N 36°55.928'/ E 24°42.309'). Further on you notice a wall on the lower

2.35   side, which later has a **gateway**.

> *Short cut:* By passing through the gateway, you come down to the road where buses pass.

Uphill to the right, with a fence on the left, you come to

2.45   the small deserted **Profítis Elías monastery** ② looking out over the plain of Platís Gialós, above which towers the large monastery of Panagía toú vounoú. Inside the chapel you can see the old icon of a black madonna.

The onward route to the valley starts at the rear of the building with the three windows. Yet more juniper bushes, some of them the size of trees, to crown the tour*.

3.05   Down in the valley you walk past a round **pen**, proceed downhill along a dirt track and a concrete track and on to

3.20   **Platís Gialós** bus station.

---

*Tonight you will simply have to find out whether there is such a thing as gin "made in Greece".

⑱ The Mycenean Acropolis

Besides the Elias monastery it is the summit church of Saint Andrew which dominates the centre of Sífnos. Not many people realize that a huge acropolis used to stand there in prehistoric times. Following paths and mule tracks, we set out to explore the green central part of the island, also visiting the excavation sites on the four-hour hike. No wateringplaces exist on the entire route.
■ *8.5 km, difference in altitude 240 m, moderate*

AWT Follow walk 19 or 20 as far as the **turn-off to Profítis
0.35 Elías** (P: N 36°44.387'/ E 25°18.372').
From there you continue on the same level, soon picking out the Eustáthios chapel above the valley covered with oleander bushes ①. In front of a sharp-cornered wall you follow the sign "Ag. Stathis" to the left. After a slight in-
0.40 cline up to a **fork** you walk on up to the right. A little later, first walk to the left of a wall, then proceed through juniper bushes until you reach the **chapel Agios Eustáthios** (P: N 36°57.338'/ E 24°42.785'). It is locked up, not even offering a pail for the cistern. Still one is pleased to find the peaceful spot amidst the green landscape, above which tower Profítis Elías on the left and the acropolis plateau on the right, hiding St. Andrew's church behind. Likewise somewhat concealed from view is the taxiarchis (archangel) church down in the valley.

Immediately above you, beside the Eustáthios chapel, you will find the path which continues on through the bushes. To the left lie fields in the valley, watched over by the

Anargýri chapel. Already now one can sense the size of the plateau above it on the right ②.
Soon you are joined by a field wall on the left, at the end of which it is only possible to make out the path with some difficulty. You walk past a couple of large boulders and head towards a saddle, the valley bottom on your left. Further on you walk immediately to the left of a field wall, then immediately to the right of the wall, which en-
0.55 closes a **field in the saddle**.

> *Alternative: Before* reaching this walled-in field one can go left and, after a gateway, climb uphill without a path towards the St. Andrew plateau ③. Higher up, however, the former path is overgrown with juniper bushes and right at the top one has to scale the fence surrounding the excavations. Altogether quite a challenge.

If you prefer it simpler, turn off to the left downhill *after* the walled-in field in the saddle. (To the right this path leads to the monastery of Aglos Nikoláos t'acrina, ⑩.) The clearly visible path runs round Mount Andrew, affording magnificent views out to sea and along the island's coastline. Above you can now discern St. Andrew's monastery ④. Where the trail subsequently drops down, you keep
1.05 left on the same contour and come to a **footpath** which
1.15 gradually winds its way up to the **Agios Andreas monastery**.

> *The double, rampart-reinforced wall encircling the acropolis was built in the late-geometrical period (8th century BC). 500 years earlier a Mycenean settlement had already existed here for 100 years. So far the ground-plans of about ten houses have been exposed. The ongoing ex-*

Apollonía – Agios Andreas – Apollonía 71

cavations will surely reveal further details. The monastery was constructed in the 16th century, mainly using stones taken from the ancient walls, much to the displeasure of the archaeologists.

1.30 From the monastery you take the steps leading down to the **road**, where you go to the right for about 120 m and then to the left along a sand track. 70 m on you turn on to a mule track, also on the left. This sweeps elegantly past a chapel (right) and down to the hamlet **Simbópoula**.

Before reaching the first houses you walk left along the dirt track which later, concreted over, runs downhill at a
1.40 right-hand bend. Exactly there you turn off to the **left** on to a wonderful old footpath which first snakes round a small valley, then rises and leads past a chapel (left) to the road. The path continues on the other side until it comes
1.55 to the **edge of Katavatí**.

You are now on familiar ground again: below the village church you go right and, at **Apollonía** grammar school,
2.10 left down to **heroes' square**, Platía Heróon.

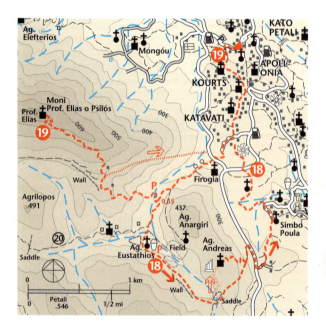

72 **Sífnos**

⑲ Elias the tall one

The steep 400 m ascent to the highest monastery on Sífnos is rewarded by a stunning view. The three-hour trek can be combined with tour 20.
■ *9.5 km, difference in altitude 515 m, moderate to difficult*

▷ *Map see left*

AWT 0.00 From the **Platía Heróon in Apollonía** (175 m) you go down the road to Kamáres for two minutes and, immediately after the water ditch (opposite the car park), up a few steps. From here the alley in the Kourtsoúdi district leads straight on uphill: pay no attention to turn-offs to right

0.05 and left. You only go right at a **junction**. Shortly after that a new chapel can be seen on the left behind a wall, while you continue uphill in the direction of a large domed church. 50 m before this church you go left and come to a slight **hollow**.

0.10 At the edge of the village of **Katavatí**, which soon appears, you keep left, coming to a transverse road, where you turn right uphill. Soon afterwards you bear left below the domed church (p. 75 ①) and follow the village street. Rising up to the right is our destination, the mighty mountain of the Profítis Elías. Next to the route on the left is the Hotel "Galini", a little later on the right a chapel with an elegant memorial slab in the forecourt.

100 m further a sign points the way to the right, which subsequently becomes a monopáti leading down to the

0.25 **by-pass road**.

Apollonía – Profítis Elías 73

Cross this on a slant to the right, where you hit upon another mule track leading uphill above a valley (right), 0.35 which takes you into the interior of the island. **The turn-off to the right** to the Profítis Elías lies in the bottom of the valley ① (**P:** N 36°44.387'/ E 25°18.372', 250 m).

It is not difficult to find the path through mastic and juniper bushes. The concrete repairs to the path, while well-meaning, were hardly workmanlike and will only last 0.50 a few years. Next to the path on the right is a **refuge** (390 m), from where you can see the Elias monastery again. Twelve minutes later is the path going off to the right which you could use on the way back. After passing 1.05 a **cowshed** (right), you notice it gets flatter before becom- 1.20 ing steeper again on the ascent up to the **monks' fortress** o.w. (680 m) ②.

> *The monastery of the **Profítis Elías o Psilós** ("the tall one"), which now stands empty, was probably founded in the turmoil of the iconoclasm around the year 800. The present-day buildings were erected around 1650. It is assumed that there was already a watch-tower here during antiquity. This highest point already served to defend the island in those times. The centre of the rectangular complex is formed by the kathólikon, the detached church. It possesses an interesting iconostasis made of stone, into which the illustrations are inserted.*
>
> *On the outside of the building, below the monastic cells, are casements with embrasures. In the other building are the refectory with a long stone table, a cistern and further embrasures. Unfortunately the cooking utensils are no longer complete, so one cannot accept the posted invitation to coffee.*

To return, use the same way, possibly taking the short cut to the north (AWT 1.00) or joining ⑳.

🟠 At the Foot of the Prophet

This four-hour route is easy to follow and leads through a sparsely cultivated area to a valley at the foot of Profítis Elías. For relaxing at the end of the trek, taverna chairs on the sand and the beach of the quiet bay of Vathí await us.

■ *9 km, difference in altitude 420 m, moderate*

AWT	
0.00	The day begins at the **main square in Apollonía**, at the passage next to the cake-shop which leads into a narrow alleyway. After 40 m you bear right, up the main alley. The boutiques are still closed and the chairs of the tavernas upturned. Yet a few people are already having their breakfast. During the week all the churches are closed, in-
0.05	cluding the large **Metropolis Church** (left). At the upper end of the stair-path head right for a few metres along the asphalt road, leaving it again at the signpost to Katavatí.
0.10	You go left below **Katavatí church** 1, then on past the
0.15	hotel "Galini" (left) and the church of **Panagía Angelokísti**, in whose forecourt lies the epitaph of a pope. At the fork, 80 m further on, signposts point right towards Mt. Elias. You head straight on downhill over concrete, then
0.20	through an olive grove on a monopáti to the **bypass**, which you follow right for 50 m before climbing up some steps (sign "Elias"). Not much can go wrong from here on, and there are blue marker dots into the bargain! The wall-lined track you now use 2 lies on the slope opposite Mt. Elias. First comes a turn-off to the left to Anargýri
0.35	chapel, then, in the hollow, the **trail** to Profítis Elías turns off to the right. (**P:** N 36°44.387'/ E 25°18.372').

Apollonía – Katavatí – Taxiarchis tis Skafis – Vathí

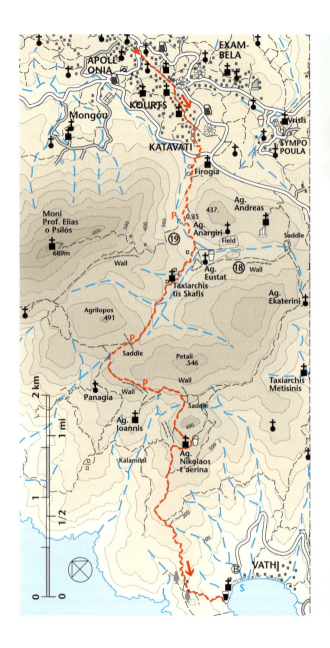

Our route continues straight on here. Later, in front of a wall (sign: "Stathis") below a chapel ③, it turns right up into a high valley, where the Archangel and his church,
0.45 **Taxiarchis tis Skafis** ④, soon appear amidst some ruins. If it is open, you can see some beautiful, though badly damaged frescoes in the chancel, or bema. Some of the monastery terraces in the valley are planted with vines, watched over from above by the fortified monastery of the Prophet Elias. Above the eastern/left-hand end of the valley you can make out the flattened excavation site near the St. Andrew's monastery, though the monastery itself cannot be seen.

1.00 Attractive steps lead on to the **pass**, from where Mílos and Kímolos are visible. 20 beyond the gate in the saddle (**P:** N 36°57.340'/ E 24°41.966', 390 m) you go left at the fork and again at the next one. You are led left uphill by a concrete path, which becomes a reddish gravel track near a
!! wall. Now you have to be careful: 30 m above a wall, *on a*
1.15 *ledge of rock*, a **narrow path** forks off the wider one *to the left* (**P:** N 36°57.240'/ E 24°41.725'). We take the narrower of the two, which runs up above and parallel to the larger one, and follow the contour lines, our eyes fixed on the white, domed church ⑤ which lies on the right, below the next peak. Coloured dots and cairns line our route. A huge crevice is visible on the opposite slope. Which one of the Greek Gods raged here? The mule track brushes the
1.25 **walls** on the left of the pass, and follows round the curves of the next hill, keeping at the same height. At a fork on the left of a wall you veer left. The track winds on ahead
1.35 through juniper bushes to **Agios Nikoláos t'aerina** monastery, in whose forecourt there is a water tap. If you

Apollonía – Katavatí – Taxiarchis tis Skafis – Vathí   77

don't want to wait and have your picnic under olive trees in twenty minutes' time, the best place to stop for a rest is the roof of the toilet building. The day's goal, Vathí with its attractive bay, is visible down below.

The way there begins between the monastery and the small building mentioned above, running down a slight incline. Soon another path coming down from the right joins our track. Some more dots appear, pointing the way ahead to the left. We stay left of the fissured mountain, moving on over broken stones and through juniper bushes. The Elias mountain monastery is again visible from here. You can choose among the extremely pleasant sites to have a picnic in the walled fields ahead!

2.15 The well-marked track 6 first leads down towards the sea, then down to the bay. In **Vathí** the taverna "Tsikali" with its chairs on the sand awaits us!

The narrow sandy beach is right next door. To reach the bus, you have to walk 100 m inland. The last bus leaves relatively early in the spring, and as late as midnight in the high season.

㉑ The watery monastery

Far away from everything, at the island's outer extremity, stands a little monastery. This five to six-hour walk leads there on narrow tracks skirting Mount Elias and then over the mountain ridge and down to the sea. Along the route are two further monasteries. Water can be drawn from cisterns at two places. To shorten the walk you could try to find a fisherman to fetch you from Vlasí beach.
■ *13 km, difference in altitude 300 m, difficult*

AWT As always we start from the tree-lined heroes' square in
0.00 **Apollonía**, where the road to Kamáres runs downhill for
0.02 200 m. Opposite the **car park** (right) we swing left and ascend the steps leading up to a lane. But we turn off this to the right after only 30 m, at a power pole, and proceed along a monopáti. On the next hill is the cemetery which we will be passing again later. At the next fork we go right
0.05 and come to an **asphalt road**, which we cross diagonally to the right.

After that our route heads right, past some houses and down through the bed of the stream, then to the right of the "homely" dovecotes ① and uphill along a rocky
0.10 monopáti to the **cemetery**. Dead easy, the walk can go on like this for ever!

From the cemetery we command a view of what is still to come ②: our first goal is the monastery with the blue dome on the left in the foreground, the next one is the more distant monastery with the antennae up on the mountain. The route looks more difficult than it is!

Apollonía – Panagía tósou neroú – Apollonía/Kamáres

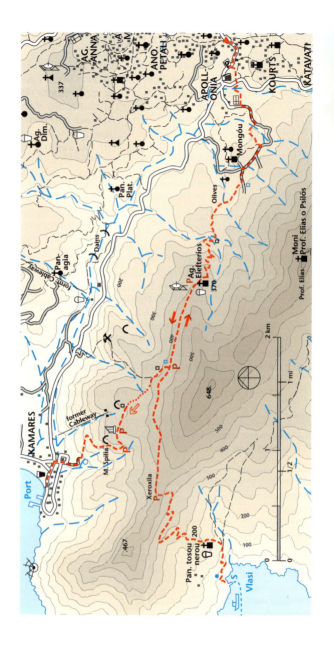

80 Sífnos

      The gravel path starts off level, veering left, then slightly uphill. After 200 m we take the second mule track on the right and, walking up through olive groves, rejoin the now familiar gravel path. We walk along it to the right and then down to a crossing, where, after passing through
0.25 the portal, we turn right down to the former **monastery Theológos ton Mongóu**.

> *The 400-year-old monastery used to accommodate society ladies who failed to live up to the reputation of their families. It is now in private ownership. Nevertheless, visitors are still most welcome to have a look round the church with its very beautiful "baroque" iconostasis.*

      Back at the crossing above the portal we go straight on up the dirt track. 20 m before a water reservoir we are relieved to discover a wall-lined path on the right heading towards our goal on the mountain. Further on some clumsi-
0.40 ly repaired steps lead up to **ruined houses** (left). 80 m
!!   after these we turn *sharp left* beside high walls.
0.55 More steps lead up to the vacant **monastery Agios Eleftérios**. Inside the plain church the visitors' book reveals when the last hikers passed through here. We have a choice between water from the cistern or ouzo at the guesthouse. It still exists, filoxenía, Greek hospitality. Unfortunately, though, it is too early for a swig from the bottle!

      We have to move on – past the radar reflectors on the right (**P:** N 36°58.604'/ E 24°41.936'), along the slope ③. Below the path can be seen the upturned brown masses from the ore mining and a cavernous pit. Standing guard on the mountain range opposite, above the Kamáres valley, are the summit monasteries of the prophet Elias (left) and Saint Simon.

Apollonía – Panagía tósou neroú – Apollonía/Kamáres

1.10 In the meantime we have reached a **reservoir** (**P:** N 36°58.734′/ E 24°41.323′) on the right-hand side of the path, serving as a point of reference. From here a path drops down to Kamáres which we can use later. But first we stay on the previous path and enjoy the distant views of the countryside and sea.

1.25 Later we come to the mountain crest of **Xeroxíla** (**P:** N 36°58.719/ E 24°40/713′, 420 m), which means "dry wood". Understandably – up here it blows like in a wind tunnel. Before we dry out ourselves, we had better leave
★ the windy saddle. A superb view of the island opens up: in the background the lofty Mílos, in front of it Kímolos, to the left of it Poliégos, on the right in the sea the block formed by Antimílos. But a monastery? None to be seen anywhere.

Only after proceeding along the difficult, slippery path for some time do we see it down below. The trail gradually
1.50 winds its way down to the unoccupied **monastery Panagía tósou neróu**, to the "Mother of God of the many waters" ④. A welcoming spot. The church is plain and the rooms inviting: a long table and a kitchen.

> *Bathing:* Right beside the monastery a few steps run down to a path which meanders on down through rocks before joining another path which would lead left along the southern slopes of Mount Elias to Apollonía. Turning right here, you come to **Vlási pebble bay** ⑤ after a quarter of an hour.

1.50 It is reluctantly that we take our leave of the welcoming **monastery** and climb on up the familiar path. In the
2.25 **saddle** the meltémi blows our hat off again, while saint Simon smiles across from the other mountain range.

Further along the path, down to the left, it is possible to see the roughly six metre high rectangular towers erected closely together at the top station of the old material cableway belonging to the ore mines.

The alternative route to Kamáres runs about 80 m ahead of these towers. On the flat hill to the left of them, on the right above Kamáres, can be detected the round stone surface of an ancient watch-tower; this trail also goes past it, before dropping down on the left of the mountain.

2.40 Soon we return to the **reservoir** and have to make a decision.

For Apollonía take the now familiar track back as far as
2.55 **Agios Elefterios monastery**. In front of the monastery you see Apollonía in the mild evening light. Now is surely the time to sit down outside the guesthouse for a bit – and try that ouzo after all. Yet Apollonía beckons, so better press on ... and eschew the bottle!
3.20 Walking first past **Mangóu monastery**, we return to
3.45 **Apollonía** on well-beaten paths, arriving back at the heroes' square, only the heroes are now rather tired.

Alternative route to Kamáres

Only experienced hikers should attempt this route. The upper, level part calls for orientation skills, while the following steeper descent requires a certain degree of sure-footedness.

2.40 At the **reservoir** descend about 10 m further down to the left of the low country wall, where you find a path hea-

ding to the left. It forks near a ruined house (right) – we take the left branch-off, which leads to the next hill with another ruin. Walk straight on past these ruins (on the right is a deep hole from the ore mines), later passing the

2.55 two precisely stacked pylons of the old material **cableway** 80 m over to the right ⑥.

On the left above the entrance to the harbour is a string of mountains with *three peaks*. Taking the right-hand (lowest) peak as a bearing, head in that direction through a slight hollow. Cairns help to locate the track, which leads

3.00 past the round **ancient signal tower** (**P:** N 36°58.982′/ E 24°40.983′). With a diameter of ten metres, it is only one metre high now and has two entrance stones ⑦. The remains of 55 such antique towers may still be found on Sífnos. They served to transmit alarm signals in the event of danger.

Standing at the entrance stones, now take a bearing on the *middle* mountain peak. More cairns line the way along the admittedly rather obscured track through the juniper thicket. Several tracks run almost parallel. At an incline, with a view of Kamáres (**P:** N 36°58.973′/ E 24°40.903′), you first stumble across the old rock path heading downhill and then reach steps which have been laid to take one

3.10 in to the large **cave** *Mávri Spiliá* to the right above the track.

✓ From here on the path is littered with loose stones and requires sure-footedness ⑧. After 100 m the most difficult passage has been overcome and, at a right-hand bend, you reach some wide steps which give an impression of how wide the original track must have been. Take a final break to relish the end-of-day panorama.

A little further on the former track is somewhat overgrown, so it is advisable to use the colour-marked short cuts down to the left. The path then crosses a scree slope,

3.20 makes a **left-hand bend** and drops down to the round re-
3.30 servoir, where it becomes a dirt track leading to **Kamáres**.

Sífnos 85

Anáfi

The most south-easterly island of the Cyclades is isolated and mountainous. It consists of gneiss, quartzite, marble, mica schist and sandstone. which were thrust to the surface here at the seismic arc (p. 10). During the earthquake of 1956 Anáfi experienced the same devasating fate as Santoríni.
The isolated island remained largely uninhabited for some 200 years due to marauding pirates and even today is barely cultivated. How reassuring to know that the island is supposed not to have any snakes.
For many years the island remained unaffected by mass tourism. But this could change thanks to several very beautiful sandy beaches. Anáfi is certainly worth the short sea crossing.

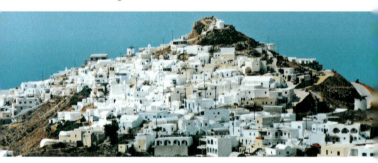

㉒ The green heart

Like many Greek islands, Anáfi appears to be rugged and rocky from the sea. Yet in the middle are green valleys – at least in spring. The three-hour circular tour takes us through hilly countryside, partly on old paths. Along the way, though, we encounter neither tavernas nor wells.
■ *5.5 km, difference in altitude 140 m, easy to moderate*

AWT At the bus parking place in **Chóra** you turn off the road to
0.00 the left beside the quaint chapel and the antenna and

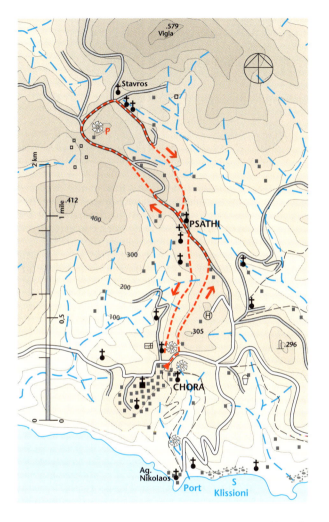

then pass two windmills (left). This is where an old mule track begins, running north along the edge of the slope. After a bend you see the helicopter pad up on the top of the mountain.

0.15 When you come to a wide **dirt track**, you go left and soon reach the few houses in Psáthi, above which towers

a chapel on the right. Take a final glance back at the fantastically situated Chóra, stretching out above the sea.

The dirt track winds sharply to the right, but following the remains of the old mule track you go *straight* ahead, climbing slowly until you rejoin the dirt track. Now go
0.40 left as far as a holiday house. The (fake) **windmill** (**P:** N 36°22.090'/ E 25°45.779') standing above it is, at 380 m, the highest point on the tour and makes a good resting place.

At the house you continue in the same direction *on the upper track*, go round the windmill hill and soon see the
0.50 Stavrós chapel standing below **Mount Vígla** 1.

Before you get there is a **cross-roads** (cross = Greek "stavrós"), where right up until a few years ago several mule tracks converged.

★ Hiking to the right or south-east, then above two chapels standing to the left of the trail, you appreciate the panoramic view across the island's green heartland, with its patchwork of fields, chapels and little houses. At the end of the dirt track begins a narrow path 2 which later affords even better views over as far as Mount Kálamos. This path runs above a wide valley and brings you back to
1.10 the already familiar **dirt track** near Psáthi.

Go left along it, but leave the wide track after only a short while at the crossing below the chapel. (If you want to take things a little easier, you can also return along the already familiar track.)

Below the dirt track is a rather overgrown mule track and beside that a path which is easier to negotiate. This runs
1.35 along the hillside, past a tiny chapel and back to **Chóra**.

88   Anáfi

23 Ancient Anáphe

This five-hour circular walk leads through hills to the remains of the ancient town of Anáphe and then on down to the sandy beach of Roukónas, where you can stop at a taverna. You return to Chóra along narrow paths above the coast. Water and perhaps food should be taken along, as the cisterns en route do not seem to be particularly trustworthy. If you intend to return from Roukónas by bus, you should ask for the times in the morning.

■ *10 km, difference in altitude 280 m, moderate*

AWT 0.00 From **Chóra** you take the road leading down to the port and turn up left after about 350 m. Then you bear right down to the gravel/lime works, above which a dirt track

0.15 leads up left towards a **double chapel**. You pass to the left of it and find yourself first on an old sunken path leading downhill, later on a dirt track. At the end of the valley you come past a farmhouse. You walk round the cactus-cov-

0.25 ered valley, before turning right down the **dirt track** at the fork. Very soon you see a farm shed below the track, still above the green valley bottom, which you will pass on walk 24.

But we continue a little further along the dirt track, find a path going right across the valley bottom and stride on

0.30 uphill between two **houses** 1. After two minutes you veer right, climbing to the right of the hill. After another two minutes you keep left uphill. After a small saddle with olive trees and a ruined house we notice a green hollow below right and, behind it, a wide mountain ridge with a

Chóra – Anáphe – Roukónas – Chóra   89

0.45 marker post in the middle. To the left of it you reach a **saddle** ② (arrow) along trails.

Above the next valley is Kastélli mountain, to the right of whose peak once lay the ancient town of Anáphe. We meander down along mountain trails, first left, then right to the baking-oven and from there to the intersection between two valleys marked by a small farmhouse ③. The
1.05 house on the **valley floor** stands in a small garden with vines, lemons and pomegranates.

Leaving the house and climbing a few steps up into the right/eastern valley, after the rocks in the gully outside the garden, we discover the continuation of the trail to the rigth on the opposite slope. The path runs past some
1.25 ruins and a stable up a slight incline to the **Chapel of Docári Panagía** ④ (**P:** N 36°21.313'/ E 25°47.914'). In front of it a well-preserved sarcophagus has found its present resting place, very likely having been put to use as a cattle-trough. Griffons, the horse Pegasus and six Cupids are depicted.

1.35 *After a ten-minute climb, to the right of the summit, we are now standing among the few remains of the **Dorian town of Anáphe**, built around 800 BC. It was abandoned after Roman times, about 500 AD, probably because of an earthquake. At the time a processional road led from here to the temple of Apollo in Kálamos. Up to 1998 exquisite marble statues from the Roman period were found on the site. They were partly damaged in a clearance fire and are now on display at the museum in Chóra.*

Passing the chapel again – and a few ruined houses – on narrow paths, we head down towards the sea. On the left

90 **Anáfi**

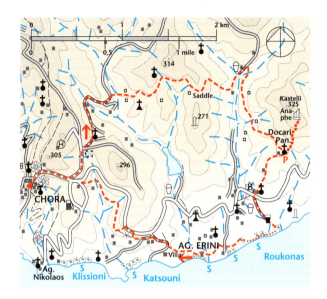

we see another chapel and cairns on a rocky ledge above the sea. In ancient times such cairns acted as signals for the ships, which were then pulled onto land in Anáphe port down below. On the site today is the dream strand of **Roukónas** and a taverna which is open in the summer from June.

★
2.10

At the western end of the long beach, in the dry valley, start paths which run along the coast to a large fenced **holiday villa**, from where a wide track leads uphill. (If you go left at the perimeter fence, you drop down to the bay of Katsouni.)

2.30

2.35 Up at the **fork** below the road you go left along the wide path and then, after 80 m, right along a narrow path which is later interrupted by roadworks. So you have to climb up to the road, but already after 100 m, at a concrete culvert, you can return to the path running parallel
3.10 below and march on to **Chóra**.

Chóra – Anáphe – Roukónas – Chóra 91

㉔ Kálamos Marble Cliffs

From May to September you can use the bus for part of this eight-hour tour and thus give yourself more time for a swim. The route mainly leads along the coast, passing several cisterns and a taverna. Very attractive and, in part, empty beaches are ideal for bathing. These alone make the tour worthwhile.
■ *20 km, difference in altitude 210 m, difficult*

AWT We follow the route description of walk 23 up to the dirt track above the valley floor (AWT 0.25).

Short cut: if you want to save 10 min., continue down the main road leading to the port for about 100 m from the fork until you reach the metal signs ("Kastélli") and follow them by turning left on to the footpath along the coast. This path joins the path described below at AWT 0.55.

0.25 From the **dirt track** you walk to a farm shed down to the right, still above the valley bottom. To the left of the shed you go down to the valley bottom. Trails run first to the left, then to the right of the dry stream-bed; follow them out of the valley as far as the new reservoir, where you continue along a dirt track leading to a road, which you take up to the left.

Having passed a hilltop chapel (right), you go through a gate on the right and proceed down the dirt track leading
0.55 to the ruins of the hamlet **Agía Eríni** and further down into a green valley. This is crossed by the old monopáti which you will be coming down from the left on the way back. The marble cliffs of Kálamos can now be seen ①. We

92 **Anáfi**

★
1.10

head towards the sea and, in front of the beach house, continue left across the hill on a marked path. The next beach (without a house) is part of the long dream strand of **Roukónas** with its fine sand and, further inland, a nice taverna.

1.25

At the end of the beach you climb up to man-sized cairns and on to a small chapel assembled with parts from ancient buildings. Similar cairns served as markers for the port of the ancient Dorian town of Anáphe. Behind the chapel, among green marble and mica schist, is a path leading up right to the old **main path**, which you now follow to the right along the coast.

A steep-sided valley reveals holiday houses next to a mini-windmill with gaily turning sails. The path continues precipitously above the sea, soon looking down upon a whole series of sandy coves and up to the large monastery. After passing the monastery gardens, you end up in front of a locked gate – if you haven't picked up a key on your way through Chóra.

2.20

The abandoned **Monastery of Zoodóchos Pigís**, *the "life-giving source", is 200 years old and was built on and from the ancient ruins of an Apollo temple* 2. *Ancient recycling, the archaeologist's nightmare. This temple has its origins in the realm of Greek legend. The Argonauts, who stole the Golden Fleece from the "Eldorado" of Colchis on the east coast of the Black Sea, first set foot on Greek land again here after a stormy sea journey and, out of gratitude, set up an altar on this site which subsequently became a temple.*

The rest of the route to the summit first leads past a semi-ancient chicken run and then becomes an easily identifi-

✓ able path up the mountain ridge. A good head for heights is essential at the top, as steep inclines ③ have to be overcome before we can finally enjoy the view from the sum-
3.20 mit, from **Panagía Kalamiótissa**, the patron saint of the island, to well beyond Crete; but visibility often only extends as far as the island of Pacheiá, Greek for "the fat one".

The summit church was rebuilt in 1956, having been destroyed during the immense earthquake. Over the past 400 years several churches have been built on this spot. Monks are also supposed to have lived here earlier. Up until a bad accident caused by lightning more than 100 years ago, the Anáphians used to trek up here for the church celebrations each year! Nowadays they only drive to the monastery on the mountain below.

The attractive site of the monastery ④ on the way back down may remind some of the descent from Mount Sinai to the Monastery of St. Catherine.

4.10 Passing the **monastery**, you take the same route back down to the beach. Timetables permitting, you can also ride back in the bus. Times were it was a lot prettier, though: you could take a kaíki back. Before setting off, be sure to take some of the delicious spring water in the monastery gardens. At the fork above the cairns you go
5.15 right. Above the taverna at **Roukónas** the path merges with the road which goes round the valley. The bus stops here. The old, now sadly overgrown path runs in the hollow on the left.

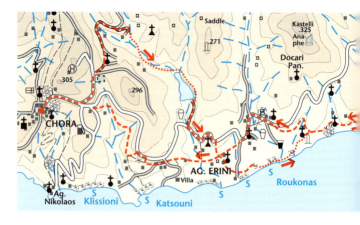

94 **Anáfi**

Above the next valley a dirt track turns off to the left. Just past the barrier chain you will be relieved to rediscover to the right the old carved out path which now continues without interruption. Above small holiday houses you take the dirt track which runs parallel below the road.

Shortly afterwards a footpath branches off up to the right.
5.45 Where this later becomes impassable, use the higher **road** for a minute. When you see red markings at a concrete culvert, climb back down to the path and enjoy the walk
6.15 round the valley until you reach **Chóra**.

▶ From **Chóra** to the **beach of Klissióni**. A trail leads from the last guest-house at the end of the village, below the road, to two chapels and then down the hill opposite Chóra to the road. After a short stretch you reach the road leading to Klissióni.

To reach the **Katsoúni beach**, follow the road to the port for about 500 m and, at the signs to Kastélli, turn left on to a path, then right again downhill.

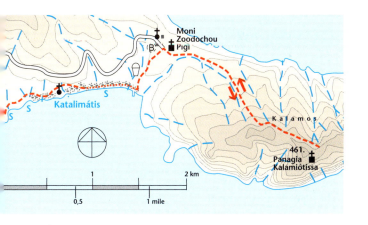

Folégandros

Exposed to stormy weather, the island consists of marble in the east and schist in the west. The eastern part is scarcely farmed and very barren. In the western part on the other hand the agricultural terraces continue to be tilled. That is where old mule tracks can still be found – and the reason why the following walk is surely the finest on the island. DEMO has produced a good Greek map of the island on a scale of 1:25 000 which is available everywhere, although it does not always show the footpaths accurately.

㉕ A lonely strand

Away in the west lies a lonely bay which is only accessible on foot: it takes four hours to reach plus another hour up to Ano Meriá, from where the bus heads back to Chóra. Be sure to obtain the bus timetable before setting out.
The very beautiful walk exclusively follows mule tracks, but does not offer anywhere to stop, only a well. So ...
■ *15 km, difference in altitude 260 m, difficult*

AWT As far as Stavrós Chapel the beginning of the trek is identical with walk 26.
0.15 20 m beyond the **Stavrós Chapel**, with a bounce in your step, you saunter right on to a roadway which soon leads
0.20 past three **windmills** ①. Continue a few metres along the contour lines, then downhill to the right after a goat pen.

| | The narrow path runs daringly along the steep coastline |
| 0.25 | until you once more come up to a chapel on the **road**. |

Go down this road to the left for 80 m, leaving it again to the right after Paraskévi chapel, where an old path leads down into Angáli valley. From the path you can soon pick out the buildings on the bay. Having passed a couple of houses to the right of the path, you cross a concrete road

0.40 near two **wells**. (The upper well has good water.)

Diagonally opposite, 15 m further up to the right and somewhat concealed, are a few steps leading on uphill. Our mule track runs along the side of the slope, Angáli on the left. (On the right a steep path soon leads up to Ano Meriá.) We wander on effortlessly, following the contour lines, and even sing a little song. Later, however, the route climbs steeply to the right of some olive trees, then becomes more leisurely again as far as the abandoned hamlet **Georgi**

0.50 **t'Aga**, where a palm-tree stands. 50 m beyond it another path leading up to Ano Meriá branches off – here too we go straight ahead, but down left after 80 m.

Walking along above the coastline, you notice the holiday lets on Galifos bay which, with their paraffin lamps in the evenings, still promise true romanticism. Later you look down on Agios Nikoláos bay with the tamarisks.

The descending track becomes narrower – in the course of the years it has been trodden into the slate. Before the ru-

1.00 ins of the hamlet Mármaro the **path** turns off to Agios Nikoláos bay, but this should *not be taken*. It takes seconds to stride through Mármaro, before dropping down into a hollow ②, above which a chapel stands watch. Below you

1.05 rather murky water gathers in a **pool**, albeit in a bed of noble marble.

Chóra – Angáli – Livadáki – Ano Meriá   97

Regrettably the route climbs yet again, and rather strenuously too – on a path across eroded rock. Afterwards it crosses a strung-out olive grove, which rises up the mountain in a hollow. This is where the path ends in front of a large walled-in area measuring roughly 150x150 m. To the right of it you follow the markings leading uphill until the walls become narrower again. The track now runs horizontally above olive terraces and uphill again until it forks

1.25 **above a farm**.

Our path goes down left and, temporarily lined by walls, towards the sea. When you reach the top of the hill shortly afterwards, bear right and slowly downhill. Hugging the

1.35 hillside, the track turns right before a **field wall**. The lighthouse comes into view, beyond it Mílos. Following the wall

1.45 on the left-hand side, you come to **ruined houses**, where you continue right and uphill again.

Still with the wall immediately to the left, the path takes a broad sweep round the lighthouse, which soon lies on the port side abeam ③. In this section two walls make the path narrower, which later follows the left-hand wall downhill. About 80 m below a small area bordered by rocks you leave this wall and go right.

Now it is important to observe the dots and cairns! The track drops to the right and down to the next bay in a right-hand bend. The final stretch runs horizontally, be-

2.15 fore descending along a short red sandy path to **Livadáki Bay** ④ (**P:** N 36°38.160'/ E 24°51.547'). More than likely there isn't a soul around and you can bask undisturbed in the sun and the sea.

On the other side of the bay, beside a stone hut, a wide path leads uphill. If you look back from there, you can

98 **Folégandros**

catch another glimpse of the prominent lighthouse and the dramatic rocky coastline. The easily identifiable path ends at another stone hut (left) in front of walls and

2.30 merges with a **monopáti** at a gap.

Alternative: while this route is shorter, it takes just as long on account of the partly overgrown sections at the beginning.

To the right of the a.m. walls you descend into the valley on the right without using any tracks and up again on the other side to a wall-lined monopáti, which is easy to find, though possibly rather difficult to negotiate lower down. Once at the top, go left further uphill and left again at a fork. Keeping above a field, you come to a wide wall-lined strip of rock, which you follow uphill to the right. After passing Panagía chapel (right), you come up to **Ano Meriá**.

2.30 The more straightforward route leads past the small stone barrier on to the above mentioned monopáti and on uphill, past the ruins of a hamlet (left) and as far as the sum-

2.55 mit chapel **Anargíri**. It not only offers spectacular panoramic views, but also contains magnificent illustrations inside.

The mule track continues on up to the road leading to

3.10 **Ano Meriá-Merovígli**. In the village you walk past the bus turning place to the inn next to the Saint Andrew's chapel (**P:** N 36°38.881'/ E 24°52.146'). That is the best place to test whether the bus is punctual.

▶ Taxi: mobile 69446-93957

▶ Pasta fans will naturally want to try *matsata*, a local form of tagliatelle which is eaten both as a side-dish and as a main course.

Chóra – Angáli – Livadáki – Ano Meriá 99

㉖ Western Beaches

This four-hour circular walk along the sandy beaches of Angáli and Agios Nikoláos to the village of Áno Meriá shows the charming side of Folégandros. Easily identifiable monopátia lead through terraced fields and gardens. Shady tavernas await us on the beaches.

■ *11 km, difference in altitude 280 m, moderate*

▷ *Map see left*

AWT
0.00 From the taverna "Nikos" you stroll north out of **Chóra**, leaving the village at a flight of steps leading down beside the **pension "Seaview"**. Below the edge of Chóra a **footpath** ① makes its way high above the sea and the terraces, and below the road. Always following the contour lines, it passes the flat-roofed Sávas chapel (right) in the saddle. Beyond the following hollow begins a dirt track which, at

0.15 a sharp angle, comes to the **road**, along which we proceed to the right for 300 m. *20 m* after the Stavrós chapel (to the right above the incision in the terrain) you turn off left on to the path higher up, which later becomes a mule track.

0.20 With only one wall on the left, it leads to a **hollow** ②, above which stands the only farmhouse in the area. The paved trail leads up again and is then walled on both

0.25 sides. When the walls **drift apart** between two round walls, we follow the one on the right downhill in a wide

★ arc. Then comes a big surprise: a kalderími paved with multicoloured marble slabs runs through this mountain-

Chóra – Angáli – Ag. Nikoláos – Ano Meriá

0.30 ous area. An olive grove comes into view above the sea and this enchanting Cycladic picture is complemented by a **chapel** ③.

The idyll ends 150 m below the chapel, where you have to climb over three low fences and search for goat tracks leading to the only house further down. Below the house
0.40 to the right is the stony **Firá bay**. From here you reach the
0.50 sandy beach of **Angáli** along small paths which wind their way through boulders. During the season a taverna awaits you. But you are not always alone here.

> *Short cut:* take the oleander-lined road which leads up from the beach for about 550 m until you come across a well (left). Directly vis-à-vis on the right a dirt track swings uphill to a house, later becoming a monopáti. That is the way to Chóra, as described in the opposite direction in ㉕.

Concrete steps lead up from the beach to the tamarisk-
1.10 covered sandy bay of **Agios Nikoláos** (P: N 36°37.825'/ E 24°53.075'). Overlooking it is a panoramic café, while the fine sandy beach later offers shady trees.

After a well-earned rest we go through a gap in the wall *10 m behind* the beach house, then immediately uphill without a path (red dots). Later the walls narrow in an incision in the terrain, placing us between them, and then continue uphill on to a monopáti. Further up, to the right of the ruins of Marmaro, this merges with a mule track which runs along the side of the slope. If you follow it to the right, you come to another fork, where you go down to the right. 80 m before the ruins of the hamlet Georgi
1.30 t'Aga (with palm) you go left at a **turn-off** and rather steeply uphill.

102 **Folégandros**

Now and again we encounter a farmer who greets in a friendly manner, yet casts a worried look at our hiker's legs. Whatever do they think? We for our part have a stunning view back across the sea ④. Higher up the trail becomes flatter, a chapel on the left greets us and we arrive at the Museum of Ethnology (open from 5 pm) (**P: N 36°38.503'/ E 24°53.170'**). From there we reach the road
2.00 and walk left to the bus stop of **Áno Meriá**.

㉗ Eastern Beaches

It takes three hours to hike from Chóra to Karavostássis harbour along dirt tracks and stony paths. The trek leads through a karstic landscape, but does not require advanced orientation skills. You have several beaches to choose from, but the only tavernas are in Karavostássis.
■ *8 km, difference in altitude 300 m, easy*

AWT On the western edge of Chóra you take a few steps down the road to Ano Meriá, leaving it after a hotel complex
0.00 (left) and before the **signpost** to Angáli on the left. A concrete track leads uphill. At the fork you climb right to
0.05 a wall-lined concrete track, which becomes a **sandy track** leading to a farmhouse (right). On the left is a group of new houses. Continue straight ahead uphill, keeping left
0.10 at the **fork** in the path. You cross under a power line and pass a tall pile of stones (right).

The windsock on the hill to the left marks the helicopter landing pad. When you reach a dirt track, turn right and
0.15 then left at a fork to the flat-roofed chapel of **Deftéra Paroúsia** ① (310 m) with its cosy fittings. You proceed along the dirt track, but use a wide path downhill after the cistern near the tamarisks. Keep to the left of a wall and later left of the ditch.

Down below you see the Nicholas chapel. Bear left at a
0.25 **fork** in the path.

Alternative: the path on the right leads to the unprepossessing chapel, from where you take the dirt track to Petroússis.

0.35 Heading towards Petroússis, the path approaches the wall-lined fields in the hollow and ends at a **gap in the wall** (**P:** N 36°38.882'/ E 24°52.145'). From there you saunter across the field, open two lift gates and come to a peaceful dirt track running just above the fertile hollow. 20th August: it is not so empty here today. Heavily armed men in camouflage patrol on mopeds and in cars. The hunting season has begun.

0.45 Traverse the **crossing** below the inconspicuous village, skirting the edge of Petroússis, before heading down again towards the large Panagía mountain church in the background. Chóra cannot be seen from here.

0.50 100 m below Petroússis we turn right on to a **dirt track** which runs above an olive grove. After 100 m we turn right again and enter the realm of the monopátia. Up to the right on the nearest mountain, Profítis Elías, a barrel-roofed chapel shines like a lighthouse. The route becomes a stony, downhill path, still lined by walls at the start. These soon peter out and so we use the small church up on the right and the spent cartridge cases discarded by the hunters as orientation. The prophet remains above us to the right. The path is now rather rocky and somewhat arduous to walk along ②. At the feet of the prophet lies a village, we later notice. The way there is easy to find, becoming wider and reddish in colour. Having arrived in

1.05 the ordinary hamlet of **Livádi**, we soon reach the sea by turning left downhill at the fork.

Alternative: to the beach of **Katérgo**. Turn right at the fork on to the well-trodden path, up the hill past some dilapidated houses and then down a steep incline to the beach. Altogether you will need 60 minutes for

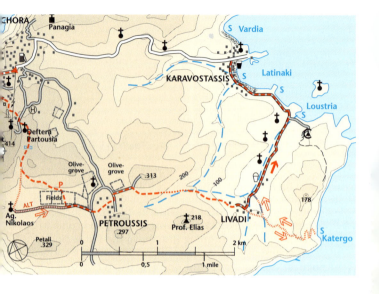

      the detour. Katérgo beach ③ is usually empty apart from the few bathers who come here by boat.
      There is *no safe way* further along the coast over to Livádi beach! If you take the same way back, you can use a red-coloured dry valley below Livádi as a short cut.

1.05 There is a wide dirt track leading from **Livádi** to the rat-
1.25 her desolate **beach** of the same name. The road then takes
1.40 us past several small beaches ④ and on to **Karavostássis**. Here you can wait for the bus in one of the many tavernas or swim at one of the two local beaches.

106   **Folégandros**

Ios

This mountainous island is composed of slate, marble and gneiss. Since the scarcity of water only permits a limited degree of agriculture, tourism provides a very welcome source of revenue. Despite the still prevalent sun-&-surf image of this "hippy" island, one can find very attractive, peaceful trails everywhere, especially in the interior of the island. Some of these have now been cleared and marked.

㉘ Beneath the prophet's antennae

Like many of its namesakes Mount Elias on Ios has now got its share of antennae as well. We will use these as reference points. The mountain's lower slopes still have old mule tracks which deserve to be reinstated. A spring can be found in a green valley and archaeological enthusiasts can also see something later on.
■ *11 km, altitude difference 330 m, easy to moderate*

AWT From **Mill Square** at the upper edge of **Chóra** you walk
0.00 uphill, with the mills soon on your left and the car park
0.05 on the right. Continue up the concrete **road** until you are led away from it to the right by the steps leading up to the Theatre O.E. You soon see the open-air theatre on your right, but pass it by. To the left of the chapel standing on the wayside you discover a rocky path which winds its way through the rocks on the right of the next chapel.
0.10 The monopáti forks after the **third chapel**.

Ios 107

	Proceed up left, where you are immediately rewarded with a magnificent view back ①. On the left you see the unmistakable Santoríni, on the right Chóra and beyond it
0.20	Síkinos. A little later you **catch sight** of the antennae of the Prophet Elías in the line of movement ②. Following a
0.25	saddle you come to a **hollow**, in the right-hand part of which are the remains of some houses. That is where you go up to the right and then left at a fork.

At a dilapidated hut the distance between the walls becomes wider – keep walking straight ahead to a saddle, from where you see wind rotors and soon afterwards the Prokópios monastery too ③, our first destination. The trail

0.35	goes slightly downhill, with a **chapel** down to the left.
0.50	Later you must not miss the **fork to the left**. It comes
!!	ten metres *before* a transversal gulley. (**P:** N 36°44.069'/ E 25°18.412', 330 m).

> *Short cut:* Parts of the trail described below are overgrown – not thorny and easily avoidable. But the easier way home is to retrace your steps on the route described above.

A goat track runs left downhill at a sharp corner, soon you see the ruin of a chapel ④. To the right of it runs a monopáti. Regrettably this is so overgrown that one has to keep to the right of it like the goats until, after a few prickly

1.00 pears, you come to a **house**.

From there a mule track runs downhill, but turns off to the left before the valley and joins a transversal path. It would be a pity not to take the detour to the right: the former **Agios Prokópios Monastery** (P: N 36°44.379'/ E 25°18,367') may be deserted, but the spring yields good water and the terraced gardens are charming.

At first you return the same way through the hollow, but then straight ahead in a south-westerly direction on an old track, although this is later overgrown in parts with mastic bushes. While these do not have any thorns, they still have to be avoided by keeping to the side. Resist the
1.20 temptation to take a right **turn-off** beside a ruin, continue straight on and put up with a little damage to the nature in order make the old path passable again. Soon the Chóra cliffs come into view again and all difficulties are forgotten. On the right-hand side in the valley you will notice a terraced hill which you may visit later on. In front of some new buildings you take the dirt track to the
1.55 right down to the **road**.

> *Alternative:* If you follow the road upwards, you come back to the mills.

If you still intend to take a swim, though, go along the road for just a short distance and then right into an alley running downhill. Further down it veers off to the right, leading out of the village to the right of some houses. As a
2.05 kalderími it leads directly to the **Skarkos archaeological hill** which was already visible from above.

> *The excavations here revealed the oldest settlement of early Bronze Age Cycladic culture. The finds date back to 2800 BC and are on display at Chóra Archaeological Museum. This site, which was abandoned in 2300 BC, once had two-storey houses, squares and streets.*

From there you follow the seaward approach, which brings you past three giant eucalyptus trees to the sports field (right). Then you go right on the road, leave it to the
2.20 left after 100 m and reach the **sea** via a dirt track.

Chóra – Agios Prokópios – Chóra   109

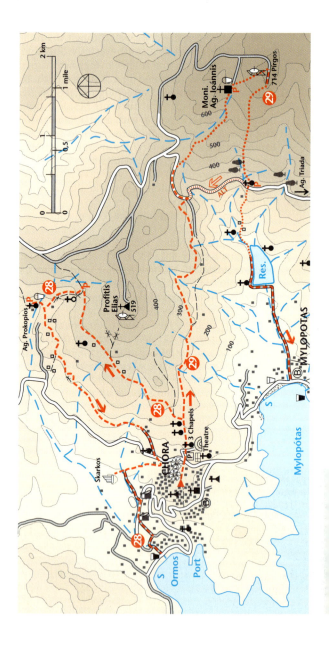

㉙ Two Mountain Peaks

In five to six hours we hike below Profítis Elías, the second highest mountain on the island, to the island's highest elevation, Mt. Pírgos, and then back to Chóra along the same attractive monopáti or over thorns and rocks to the beach of Mylopótas for a swim. Either way, we have an enjoyable break on the terrace of the monastery of Agios Ioánnis with its superb views of the neighbouring islands. The fakirs among us can negotiate the second route in short trousers.
■ *13 km, difference in altitude 580 or 714 m, moderate or difficult*

▷ *Map see left*

AWT 0.00 — To the right of the **windmills of Chóra** (135 m) we go up the concrete road, very soon realising why the mills were built on this particular site, and then follow the signs to the "Theatre O.E.".

0.05 — Some **steps** soon lead straight uphill from the concrete road to the first chapel (right). Behind it stands the new open-air theatre, built tastefully into the landscape in the ancient manner – tourism makes it possible.

0.10 — Wonderful steps lead further up and then, after the **third chapel** ①, the path forks. We head straight on, soon ending up completely alone on our attractive path. A thick water pipe is our sole companion for about 40 minutes. Ahead of us lies our goal, Mt. Pírgos and, above to the left, the mountain of the Prophet Elias: both now support a

Chóra – Moní Ag. Ioánnis (– Pírgos – Mylopótas)   111

0.20 mast. The path winds its way down to a **hollow** and, since parts of it are overgrown, it is better to walk above it.

0.30 At a right **fork** we continue left/straight ahead over wide
0.40 slabs of rock down to a **cleft** dotted with oleander bushes which is green even in summer. From here we see Mt. Elias behind us and, in front, the masts on Mt. Pírgos ②. Having passed a few houses (right), we behold the island's
1.00 latest engineering achievement – the oversized **road** to Manganári. Already 100 m before you come to it, you leave the monopáti to the right in order to get to the road. Follow this road, which is about one-and-a-half times wider than a corresponding road at home, for eight minutes. It is a relief to leave it again on the right before the left-hand bend and the steep embankment.

To the left of the green rift valley you run across the old path again. It is sometimes hard to locate, the masts provide some guidance. Approaching the saddle, down below you see a road, beehives and a green cleft. Parallel to the cleft several paths lead up the hill. Soon you see the monastery ③ up on the left. Do not cross the stream-bed too soon! Rampant heather covers every inch of the way,
1.30 but somehow we make it to the **Monastery of Ágios Ioánnis** (**P:** N 36°43.126'/ E 25°20.055').

> *Not a bad place! Looking down from the terrace we can see Profítis Elías, the protector of seafarers between Síkinos and Antíparos/Páros. Naxos, the Small Cyclades and half of Amorgós lie to the north. A temple is said to have stood here in antiquity – quite understandable with this overwhelming view!*
>
> *For our break we draw the water from the large tap in the monastery courtyard. Stone benches and tables dominate the monastery grounds, the little locked chapel rather fading into the background. During the Panigíria, the parish festival on 20th June, eating and dancing seem to be the most important preoccupations. Our two panoramic terrace tables have been reserved for 35 people. Just hope they won't all come today!*

Two different routes present themselves for the **way back**. The descent to the beach of Mylopótas is arduous. Anyone looking for an easy way home should take the same way back – this time with the fine view of Chóra.

The more adventuresome climb up from the monastery
1.45 to the summit of **Mt. Pírgos** (714 m) without a path. Here

you have a really superb view over to Santoríni, but are otherwise surrounded by rugged countryside and the hum of technology. From the viewing platform you bear right in the direction of Mt. Elias, gradually descending the slope until, half way between you and the big water reservoir, you spot a white chapel 4 directly on the road (the road cannot be seen on the photograph). This chapel is our destination.

The last 200 m are somewhat strenuous, as the terrain is overgrown. On the right you can observe how the road engineers have tormented nature, which is now taking revenge on the poor hiker. Having finally reached the chapel, you renew acquaintance with your old companion, the black pipe.

2.45 Below the flat-roofed **chapel** (**P:** N 36°42.907'/ E 25°19.355') you cross the road and, *dropping slightly*, head west towards the open sea and a few ruins, whose interiors give us an idea of their inhabitants' meager existence – hardly surprising that the younger generation has emigrated. We now climb up hill and down dale, keeping to the right towards Mt. Elias, as far as the mountain ridge. Everything is overgrown – and we search for a way down to the dilapidated houses and the olive trees on a hill above the site where the valleys converge. Once there, we wind our way down over crumbling terraces and head across a stream-
3.20 let. Below a chicken-coop we make for Mylopótas **dam**
3.40 and on along dirt tracks to the **sea**. Into the water for a swim, on the double now! The shuttle bus to Chóra runs until late evening.

Chóra – Moní Ag. Ioánnis (– Pírgos – Mylopótas)

③⓪ Two Sandy Beaches

A circular trek of three-and-a-half to four hours from an overcrowded beach to a lonely one. The first part of the route leads through cleft valleys without a trail, making orientation a little difficult. We use old mule tracks for the way back. There are no tavernas or cisterns en route. Long trousers are recommended.

■ **4.5 km, difference in altitude 80 m, easy to moderate**

AWT You take the **bus** from Chóra to the wide, busy, sandy bay of **Mylopótas** and get off at the last stop. Here we go up
0.00 left from the **hotel "Gorgona"**. Behind the houses we look for a way up. The mountain top with the TV mast should remain on our left. At the beginning it is best to take a trail some 80 m from the sea and gain height later on, as there is an impassable ditch on the shore below. We reach a saddle and come across strange retaining walls which look like stone benches. Now we should bear left uphill as it becomes flatter above. Having crossed some
0.15 **wall remains**, we can already see our destination in the distance – a small, sandy beach ①. After passing around
0.20 and down the hill, we come to a plain with the remains of a settlement. An accurately laid-out **threshing circle** ② is still well preserved.

Now continue along a path, half way up, before heading on between grandiose rocks and then turning down into a ditch. On the other side of a dry bed (red dots), we proceed up a steep incline through thorny phrýgana.

114 **Ios**

It is best to stay about 150 m below the summit. What looked like a refuse dump from the other side fortunately
0.35 turns out to be numerous white **marble rocks**: we can best continue at this height. Once around the mountain ridge, we have a better view of the sandy bay and the house ③.

We have to scramble down over the bizarre, rocky coast; later we follow the remains of a path in the ditch below. The valley is now fenced off in front of a house, but there is a way through at the water's edge. We overcome the last hurdle with the aid of the pole, and have now reached the
0.55 sandy bay of **Sapounochoma**. White arrows leading around the private house mark the way; here one doesn't disturb the guests. Now for a rest!

The way back begins behind the house and leads uphill under the electricity wires. It is marked with white dots and has a thick cover of vegetation. 50 m below the electricity cable, which runs parallel to the slope, there is an old path ④ on to which we turn left and then once again enjoy the view down to "our" bay and over towards Síkinos. Vertical stone slabs direct us like crash-barriers through the maze of rocks. The path disappears after a narrow pass, but we spot a trail of sorts on the opposite slope – here we turn up right from the top (red dots), can
1.30 see Chóra again and straight away join a **dirt road**, which we follow for 50 m before turning off right. Having gone over the pass and under the electricity wires, we notice a wide, old mule track, 80 m to the east. It leads us into the valley.

We are soon presented with a picture of rather strong contrasts – our old island trail above and the loud tourist at-

Mylopótamos – Sapounochoma – Mylopótamos   115

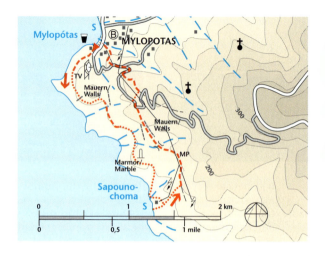

tractions below. We come back on to the dirt road, which we leave again by turning right 50 m after the fork.

A wide rock is discernible on the right below which we can use as a path. Soon we are back in the holiday world
1.50 of **Mylopótas**.

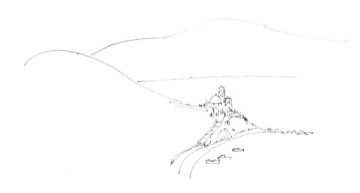

Kéa

The second largest island in the West Cyclades, also known as "Tzia", consists of marble covered by slate. One of the first islands to have been populated, it was already an important trading centre in the 2nd millennium BC.

On account of its numerous springs and wells it possesses much thicker vegetation than the rest of the Cyclades. Groves of Walloon oaks and nut trees make it an ideal island for trekking, especially as the centre of the island still boasts many charming old mule tracks which are also used.

The island administration encourages walking and, to this end, has produced a very accurate route map (red boxes inside the map above). It can be obtained free of charge in Ioulís town hall. The drawback is that some of these routes can only be covered with the aid of a taxi, as the bus timetable is not very hiker-friendly. A real treat is the "Fairy-tale Festival" in the full moon nights in July. On walks by torchlight fairy-tales are narrated in clearings (information: 22880-22400).

Of the walks described in this book, walks 32 and 34 are to be recommended in particular.

Unlike the centre of the island the coastline is rather barren. A lot of holiday houses have been built there in recent years for the Atenians who visit the island in large numbers at the weekend. The inhabitants of the island are now mainly employed in the construction industry. The catering trade and hotel business on the other hand are rather underdeveloped by comparison and tend to reach their limits on many a summer weekend. "Rooms" is a sign one hardly ever sees.

③ The Mill-Stream

"Mylopótamos" means "mill-river". Actually it is more a stream, which used to serve 13 corn mills. It can be reached from Ioulís on a three-hour trek along monopátia and kalderími. From the stream a dirt track leads on across lonely heights to the harbour in Korissía.

■ *7 km, difference in altitude 310 m, moderate*

AWT 0.00 — From the **bus stop in Ioulís** you climb up the steps to the right of the bank building. On the left you see a church after a few meters, on the right, on the other side of the valley, the old school, below which you will be passing a little later.

0.05 — After the bend comes a **well** on the left, then a chapel. From here you can see the bays of Korissía and Otziás.

Disregard the fork to the right in front of a wall, continuing straight ahead on the wonderful monopáti as far as

0.15 — the **road**.

Ascend this for about 180 m to the left, then turn right on to the concrete road. Before reaching the chapel down below on the right ①, take the path downhill. (Should it be too overgrown, you can descend without a path further to the left.)

0.25 — At the bottom you come to a **mule track** running at right angles, which you follow to the right below a retaining wall. Stay on this level, strolling along on the flat, until you come to a path which joins from higher up; go left down it. Though not very well kept, it leads directly to the

0.35 — **Constantine Chapel** ②.

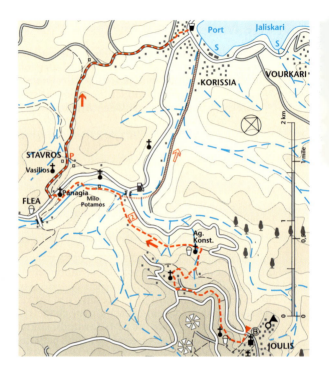

      This is where a wide paved road down into the valley begins ③. This is the middle section, the last still to be preserved, while the upper and lower parts have been covered by the road. The track marked "2" (red-and-white)
0.50 drops down into the **valley** in broad sweeps.

> ***Short cut:*** If you follow the kalderími to the right from there to the end, and cross the road, you enter the wide main valley. A dirt track takes you from there **to Korissía** in 20 minutes.

0.50 In the **valley** you leave the wide kalderími directly in front of the stream-bed to the left and veer right after 30 m, before the next house. Always keeping to the "2", we are led into a wild and romantic valley ④. We soon reach
1.00 the first of the mills, a ruin, and traverse the **stream** two minutes later. In front of a renovated mill we go right, then left immediately afterwards. A little further on we see a large round hopper with a diameter of one metre.

120   **Kéa**

This is where the water was fed into the mill. By means of a sliding valve at the bottom it was conducted on to a horizontally running water-wheel, which operated the millstones. It's long ago now ...

Next to the Panagía (Mother of God) chapel standing on the right-hand side of the path we work our way up right
1.05 to the **road**.

We march left uphill along this for about 120 m as far as the sign "Xyla", which points up right. (True "monopátists" already turn off to the right before that at the residential building, behind which they find a mule track which subsequently joins the dirt track described below.)

> *Alternative:* If you stay on the road, you come to **Fléa**, the island's largest spring, in a couple of minutes. But the detour is only worth it if you are very thirsty.

Climbing gently, the dirt track leads to the deserted ham-
1.15 let of **Stavrós** (**P:** N 37°38.521'/ E 24°18.691'). All the while we can enjoy the distant views across the fertile valley and the terraced hills.

In Stavrós we head northwest and turn our backs on the mill valley. What a contrast: the hilly landscape spread out before us is largely barren and empty. For some time we proceed above a valley lying down to the left and
1.40 eventually reach a **holiday house**. We could already make out Korissía on the right earlier on, so the next two forks do not deter us and we arrive at the harbour in
2.00 **Korissía** without further ado.

Ioulís – Mylopótamos - Korissía

32 The smiling lion

The very impressive tour leads from Chóra to Otziás in about three hours. You walk beneath holm oaks as far as the chapel Agios Prokópios, after which you pass through a romantic gorge. The paths are easy to follow and are almost entirely downhill. Food and water can be dispensed with, but not bathing togs.
■ *5 km, difference in altitude 290 m, easy to moderate*

AWT 0.00 On the **main square in Ioulís** (290 m) we take our leave of the highly decorated war hero and parade uphill, taking the steps up to the wooden signpost pointing left towards Otziás. Once outside the town, beyond the cemetery, it is already possible to make out the symbol of the island. The trail is marked "1".

0.15 *Exactly why the **Lion of Kéa** 1 smiles in such an archaic way, and turns its back on the old town in a sulk, no-one knows. One thing is for sure: despite its great age of 2600 years, and its fragile body made of slate, it has kept in good shape. It is one of the oldest monumental sculptures in Greece.*

Our onward route soon passes a large **water-well** picturesquely arranged in a semi-circle round a plane tree. Major animal markets used to take place here, the metal rings serving to tether the animals. We continue in the same direction. The main track **forks** soon after the well and down to the left you enter a quintessential Greek landscape 2 with shady oak trees. After the hollow with narrow-leaved almond trees, you walk up and come

0.25
★

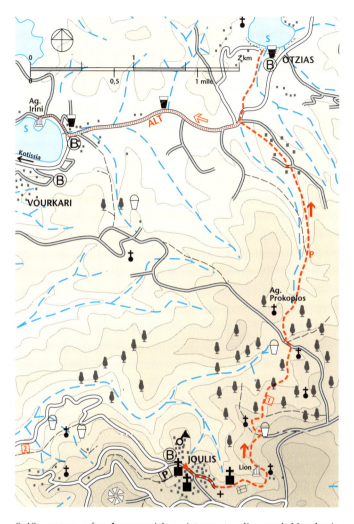

0.40 across a few **barns** with a cistern at a dirt road. Nearby is the chapel of the Agios Prokópios.

Follow the road for 80 m to the left and turn off to the right and saunter along a monopáti running down through sparse woods. Having passed bizarre rock forma-
!! tions ③, you reach the bottom of the valley. Be sure to

1.00 look out for the **turn-off** to the right a little later (**P:** N 37°39.592'/ E 24°21.210') and follow the horizontal panoramic route as far as a group of houses.

1.10 If you take the **dirt track** there for 30 m to the left, you find a mule track leading down to the coastal plain. The surrounding hills are gradually becoming covered with weekend cottages. The building regulations prescribe rough stone walls, in order to adapt to the landscape. Otziás is very popular with the Athenians.

1.20 The roadway turns into a **road**. 30 m to the right of the bus shelter is another path which drops down to the

1.25 **bathing beach of Otziás** [4].

You can sit at the shady inn here while you wait for your taxi (tel.: 0932-669493).

Should you wish to proceed on foot, the road through the isthmus is the only choice. After 20 minutes you are again standing by the waterside, enjoying the view of Vourkári. You can stop at the taverna "Mimi" and bathe behind the Iríni peninsula.

> *The **excavations on the Agía Iríni peninsula** are enclosed and, with a little luck, can be visited until 3.00 pm except Mondays. Otherwise you have to make do with peering through the fence.*
>
> *In the 1950s German archaeologists found four Bronze Age settlements which had existed here from 3000 BC until 1500 BC. A shrine was discovered here for the first time. Some of the artefacts are exhibited in the museum in Chóra.*

Continuing past the tamarisk strand of Jaliskári and all manner of holiday architecture, it takes another half hour to get from here to **Korissía**.

㉝ The windmill hill

Besides the water-mills of walk 31 the island was in the past mainly dotted with windmills. They are the first port of call on this three-and-a-half hour hike across the unspoiled centre of the island. Later we go past the remains of a fortified monastery, before returning again to Ioulís. Track-finding skills and long trousers are an asset. Along the way is one good well.

■ *7 km, difference in altitude 120 m, moderate*

AWT 0.00	Starting from the **bus parking area in Ioulís** you ascend the steps beside the bank building, at once pass a church (left) and see on the other side of the valley, as your first destination, the classical old school building. Before that
0.05	you turn up left on to a fantastic stone stairway. It leads left past a **rock chapel** and affords a final, oak-framed
0.10	view of Ioulís. After passing a chapel (left), cross the **road** and continue walking along a concrete path which runs up to the windmill hill. On the hill to the left and right of
0.15	the path are two **windmills** (weekend cottages).

Turn left here, climb over a wall 30 m further on and take the path which runs along to the left of more windmill ruins. In the background towers the unsightly accumulation of antennae on Profítis Elías.

In front of a villa you bear left down on to a somewhat overgrown monopáti and circumvent the property now
0.20 on your right. At a **fork in the path** you go right and come to the bend of a dirt track further up.

Walk right down this track until you reach a farmhouse

Ioulís – Episkopí - Ioulís 125

with a chapel on the left, where two mule tracks converge. Hence its name: Stavrós (= cross). Our route continues straight ahead and down along a narrow, shady mule track to the floor of the valley (**P:** N 37°37.989'/ E 24°20.239').

0.30 Follow the stream-bed a short distance to the right, before leaving it and climbing up left at the **fork**. This region is covered with thick vegetation and seemingly devoid of humans – apart from a chapel visible some way off on the right.

!! At the bottom of the next valley you circle round a walled-in almond grove (right) and, accompanied by walls, go uphill again. Higher up, after the entrance to a field on the right, comes our narrow *turn-off to the left* (P: N 37°37.718'/ E 24°20.319'). After about 100 m you come

0.40 to a **dirt track**, which you follow to the left.

0.45 Behind a **stone hut with gate** (right) you turn off to the right. This dirt track belongs to tour "9" of the island trails. It gently drops down into a valley, above which, a

0.50 little later, you see a dreamy **St. John's chapel** hidden among the trees up to the right ①. Ten minutes later you discover on the left-hand side another chapel in the valley ② which you can reach directly without a path or, a little later, on a dirt track which forks to the left.

0.55 Above this **St. George's chapel** (P: N 37°37.479'/ E 24°20.784') is a large enclosed rectangle with one exit. Go past it and turn up right. Without a path you keep to the left of a wall, climb up over rocks and come to the

1.00 double wall of an old, transversal **mule track** which is hardly used any more.

After clambering over the lower wall, you persevere left. The path is overgrown in parts and so long trousers are a godsend. When it later becomes almost impassable, follow the track which avoids it on the right. Later you pass the ruins of a house (right) and come to a fork. Here you

1.15 turn off to the right and soon after come to the **road**.

Go along it to the right – and discover a supermarket on the right! The land of milk and honey after all that thirsty trekking. Revitalized, we continue along the road as far as

1.20 the next **fork** to the left (sign for "Episkopí").

From here it is possible to take the "3" to the left straightaway ㉞ or to proceed along the dirt track to the

1.25 monastery of **Episkopí**.

126   **Kéa**

Only a few remains of the former fortified monastery of Episkopí are to be found, the church itself is locked up.
Walk 80 m back and then to the right down the path which is marked "3". At the fork with the wooden sign beneath shady trees you turn off to the left, at the next one
1.30 to the right ("3"), bringing you to a **well** with delicious water.
The onward route is described in ㉞, from AWT 1.50.

㉞ The ancient road

The highlight of this hike is a 2500-year-old paved road through an oak grove, which the local people call "forest". First you traverse a deserted, densely overgrown, wild and romantic region. Four hours are sufficient for this very scenic circular tour, which takes you along enchanting mule tracks and sand tracks. Along the route you will find one place to shop as well as one well.

■ *10 km, difference in altitude 240 m, moderate*

▷ *Map see previous page*

AWT Standing on the **town hall square in Ioulís** (290 m),
0.00 called a "piazza", you can see a large church looming above it. To reach the church, go up the main alley for a bit and take the first side-alley on the right. Countless ascending steps first lead you past a chapel (right), then left, and then up more steps to the right in a one-metre narrow alley. You now walk 15 m to the left, staying on the same level, and then up right again. After an occasionally roofed-over alley you go straight ahead and then up left to
0.05 the **church**.

Above that you proceed left on the same level and regain your breath. More steps! This time up to the right and then
0.10 straight on, with a twofold skew, as far as the **road** above Ioulís. Those who do not find any *stone steps* on the other side can have two more attempts, each taking ten minutes. Next to these steps is a wooden signpost with information

128 **Kéa**

on walks. We follow the local trail marked "9" uphill. After a while, on a wide expanse of rock, you come to a dirt track in front of a chapel. Turn left here, go uphill past two ruined windmills to the fork with a dirt track below a small antenna.

0.20 Bear right here. Lined up on the right-hand side are the windmills. The path runs **below holiday houses** (left) and then to the left of a farmhouse. The Elias hill to the left is dotted with antennae and wind wheels. Further down is the track which we will use on the way back.

0.25 Soon we reach the double chapel of **Agios Ioánnis & Theologos** ①. It is tawdrily furnished, but offers a quiet spot to sit in front. 50 m further on you turn off to the left in front of a stone hut and march down into the valley in the direction of the unspeakable antennae. Up to the right between the trees a St. John's chapel can be discerned, later the St. George's chapel (p. 125, ②) in the valley.

0.35 !! Whereas you pass the dirt track's **left turn-off** to the chapel, you must turn off to the left 50 m further on, on to lovely descending steps. Once down on the valley bottom, you first wander to the right, then continue along the dry stream-bed for about seven minutes. After a further five minutes a path branches off to the left, but do not take it. Shortly afterwards you see a chapel ② up to the left. Later
0.45 the path leaves the floor of the valley **below this chapel** and winds its way up to the left.

Ignore the wider path on the right leading down into the valley, instead continuing along above it until the monopáti ends near a chapel (left) and two houses.

0.55 That is where a **dirt track** to the left begins, from which the signposted trail "9" soon branches off to the right, but

Ioulís – Profítis Elías – Ioulís 129

that is of no concern to us. We allow ourselves to be led by the pleasant dirt track first on the flat, then uphill to the

1.15 **road** (**P:** N 37°36.750'/ E 24°21.230').

There we trek towards the antennae for eight minutes, turning off to the left – at a wooden signpost near a few houses – on to the wide old flagstone road. This ancient road was constructed to connect the ancient towns of Ioulís and Karthéa and has surely been improved many times since.

At the highest point (515 m) stands a wayside altar, where you continue straight on and then descend the harmo-

★ nious steps ③. Old oak trees provide welcome shade. After

1.45 a hollow you come up to the **road**. (For those who are hungry and thirsty: supermarket on the left!)

You go 80 m to the right up the road, turning left at the sign "Episkopí" and 20 m after that left again on to a mule track. (Those who wish to take a look at the abandoned fortified monastery of Episkopí stay on the dirt track (see p. 127).

Further along the shady mule track you turn off to the left

1.50 and come to a large **well** ④.

From here you follow a right-hand bend across the valley bottom and uphill. Then you must watch out: 30 m before

!! the first house on the right you have to *turn off left* in the reverse direction and continue walking uphill along a

1.55 **monopáti**. This later runs through a hollow and turns

2.05 right beside a house (left), before coming to the **road**. On the other side you continue for 100 m on the dirt track (direction "mills") and then go right on to a mule track, from where it is soon possible to see Ioulís. Having crossed the

2.10 **road** to the left, you stride along the ramp towards Ioulís and arrive – either via various alleys or more or less direct-

2.25 ly – at the **bus parking area**.

▶ Taxi tel.: 6936 660 251/6936 660 254

Kímolos

Inhabited by just 600 people, this volcanic island still offers the hiker authentic island life, many intact mule tracks through green valleys and extensive terraces for the cultivation of cereals. Kímolos possesses sufficient water supplies and agriculture is commonly practised. Instead of the ubiquitous baseball caps the farmers frequently still wear straw hats and use their donkeys. Tourist facilities are the exception rather than the rule. While there is now enough accommodation, tavernas are still scarce. The small ferry which regularly plies back and forth from Mílos permits day excursions. Together with their pupils a group of teachers has published a brochure with GPS-aided tour suggestions. "Walking on Kimolos and Polyegos" is available in the shops. A wonderful footpath leads from the harbour to Chóra (see map).

㉟ Fields and terraces

Even on a day trip this two to three-hour circular tour affords an impression of the beautiful, cultivated landscape.
The ascent up to Kiriakí chapel is rather steep and, especially in mid-summer, strenuous. Sufficient water rations and long trousers are advisable for the descent.

■ *7 km, difference in altitude 220 m, moderate*

AWT 0.00	At the **post office** (next to the telephone antenna) in the main street you go downhill, across the bridge, along the concrete path and then left. After the pension "Meltemi" you take the path going up right through terraced corn-
0.10	fields and after a fork to the right come to a **cistern**.

From there you walk along a wonderful mule track down into the valley 1, up the slope on the other side and horizontally to the left along the edge of the hill. After that you find yourself in a gully, from where you go up *right*

0.20 after 10 m. *Before* reaching a **small wooden door** (P: N 36°47.700′/ E 24°33.738′) you climb up a steep monopáti, proceed straight ahead at the first fork and right at the next one. Shortly afterwards the stone walls spread out between slabs of rock come together again and

0.35 end on **vineyard terraces** which you cross, bearing right, without a path. The dense vegetation impedes orientation – our reference point is the white, flat-roofed chapel on the mountain ridge over to the right 2 which we reach via the terraces.

0.40 The small **Kiriakí Chapel** (P: N 36°47.890′/ E 24°33.620′) is furnished in peasant style. The amusing triptych depicts the transformation of the bearded Nicholas into Saint Lucia. From the forecourt one can look across to the large, uninhabited island of Poliégos, where a monk-seal reservation is due to be created.

After the well-earned rest we continue up the hill which is about 120 m from the chapel in the direction of Poliégos. *Before* that a rather overgrown monopáti runs down to

0.55 the **valley floor** and, diagonally vis-à-vis, uphill again to
1.00 the paved **main track**.

Short cut: The way to Chóra is to the *right*.

1.10 Climbing gradually, go left along the wide kalderími as far as the **grotto-like water basin in the rock** (left). The Anargíri chapel further up the hill is closed.

1.30 Below the water basin a monopáti branches off the main track and drops down through a hollow covered with olive tree terraces. With magnificent views of Chóra (p.131) and Poliégos you descend, turn right at the fork and return to **Chóra** along a path in a deep cutting.

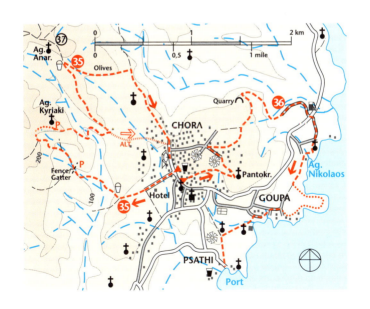

Chóra - Agios Kiriakí – Chóra 133

㊱ Cactuses and stones

This two-hour hike is also suitable for a day's outing from Mílos. It leads up to the windmill hill above the chóra, with spectacular views, and back along the coast to Psathí harbour.
■ *6.5 km, difference in altitude 120 m, easy to moderate*
▷ *Map see previous page*

AWT 0.00 The most difficult bit comes first: finding a way out of the maze of houses. START is on the **platía in Chóra**, the main square (with children's playground). Turning your back on the flagpole at the double-vaulted church, you leave the square at a slant to the right. At the first crossing go right, then left downhill. If you do not smell the bakery (right) after about one minute, go back to START or miss one round.

Keep walking straight ahead downhill until a garden wall blocks your way like a ship's bow. Go left there until another ship's bow, this time a house, divides the way, when you turn sharp left up the hill.

You've made it! The old path, lined by prickly pears ①, takes a right-hand sweep up along the edge of the hill. At

0.10 the top you go right at the **fork** to the Pantokrátor chapel, which stands on the hill like a lighthouse. The view from here is wonderful: the large, uninhabited island Poliégos on the left and two smaller islands in front of the harbour. The island in the background is the home of the Ventouris family. Island hoppers will know the name: the ferryboat owners come from here.

From the chapel you go back the same way for 50 m, then right and horizontally on to a house, where you turn off right and come to a dirt track. This runs left towards the windmills ②, which are 60 m to your left as you pass them. They are becoming dilapidated. Pity, better to invest money here than in many a superfluous traffic scheme.

Go right 10 m *before* where the concrete roads cross and before the street light.

> ***Short cut:*** Straight ahead downhill brings you back to Chóra.

The trail to the right is soon guided by walls on either side, running past a wide sliding gate into a pasture (right). That is where you go left and, at the end of the village, continue in the same direction along a track until you reach a wider path, which you take to the right. Describing a wide left-hand arc, this leads to a disused
0.25 **quarry**. Mining has been practised on the island from time immemorial; traces can be found everywhere.

At the quarry you go right down a path accompanied by a wall on the left. A stream in winter, it is correspondingly washed away and progress is slow. Your goal is the petrol station.

0.35 You first come to a **dirt track**, again beside a quarry. To
0.40 the right of the **petrol station** you cross the road and come to a gravel track running down to the seafarers' church Agios Nikoláos. On either side of the harbour lie fishing boats. Strolling down to the right, along the small **Agios Nikoláos bay**, you disappear between two walls *before* the house on the far side.

An initially narrow, then wide path runs away from the

sea. Where it leads uphill again, you can leave it to the left. It is not difficult to walk round the peninsula without a path, jumping over boulders, until you arrive in **Goúpa** ③. Colourfully painted boathouses have been picturesquely hewn into the rocks.

0.50

At the holiday houses you go right uphill before a garden wall and, where it finishes, you drop down left into a hollow with fishermen's houses. Now climb up again in their shade until where **steps** lead down to the left *before* the last house. In the next hollow you proceed before the wall of a workshop for about 200 m in the valley and then left further uphill along a dirt track ④. Up beside the chapel you join the old flagstone path leading left to **Psathí harbour**.

1.00

1.10

Rural Chapels

They are everywhere along the way, the small chapels which characterise the image of the Greek countryside. They are usually owned by farmers. The room's ceiling is either covered with flat beams or vaulted with barrel-vaults of masonry. Larger churches have a dome above a cruciform ground plan; these are called "cruciform-domed churches".

In front, a lovingly cared-for spot with a bench and often, in a tree, a bell. This is where the consecration of the church, the "Panigíri", is celebrated with singing and dancing every year on the anniversary of the church's patron saint. The relatives come from far and wide, bringing delicacies for everyone. Sometimes the hiker is lucky to turn up at the right moment. Inside, the altar wall is opposite the door, the iconostasis made of lacquered wood with icons in the compartments. The representation of the patron saint is to the right of the passage. The room behind this one is called the "Bema" and should only be entered by the priest.

㊲ The mushroom

Wandering on perfectly enchanting paths through the middle of the island we pass a natural monument, the "skiádi". From there on the trail is rather hard to find for about 10 minutes. As a reward, though, a magnificent sandy beach awaits us, where we can recover before strolling back across the fields to Chóra.
The whole tour takes about six hours. For those wishing to take a short cut and have a longer swim instead, an island taxi is ready to pick them up in Elleniká bay (tel. 6945-464093).
■ *16 km, difference in altitude 280 m, moderate to difficult*

AWT 0.00   The OTE **antenna** in the centre of the village is not difficult to find. Setting off from here, leave the village by going north along the main alley and, at a fork, straight ahead as far as the bus stop beside a power pole. Now turn

0.05   left into the **dry stream-bed**, right after the bridge and alongside the stream-bed. Before the next bridge take the path going up to the left and, proceeding outside the village, walk up a low-lying path between the fields to a

0.10   **fork**, where you go right. From here on you wander along a wide flagstone path, uphill the whole time in the direction of the radar reflector standing over to the right on the summit of Petália and serving as a point of reference. Having passed a watering-place hewn out of the rock (left), you come to Anargíri chapel, whose strange new door is unfortunately locked. 80 m further on are two

Chóra – Elliniká Bay – Chóra   137

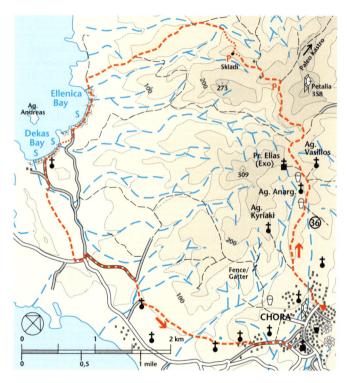

0.25 forks – go left at the **second**. Down on the right you see the lading port for bentonite – a clayey volcanic rock which is locally quarried, much less obtrusively than on Mílos. Ignore the left-hand turn up to Profítis Elías (Exo) church which you have been looking at the whole way; you will almost miss the next turn to the left. Never mind, we have to continue straight on anyway. Bear left at a fork
0.40 between some boulders, and at the next **fork** too! (Straight ahead you would come to a dirt track).

On the left lies a splendid valley, criss-crossed by the monopáti which we almost missed a few minutes ago. It
★ is possible to see the white Sarakíniko coast of Mílos ①. This breathtaking sight makes amends for the radar station up on the right.

Now comes a very important point on our route (**P:** N 36°48.593'/ E 24°32.905', 280 m), as shown by the

0.50 coloured marking arrows. The way up to the right would lead you to the old Byzantine capital of the island, Paléo Kástro (365 m), and on as far as the sea. But the ruined city has nothing much to spark the imagination of the lay visitor. So we go **left**, down to the sea.

Turn right in front of a house and left above the next (with the round threshing area). Then head for this curious mushroom-shaped stone which has been visible for some time now. At a house with threshing area you leave the beautiful, wall-lined path and cross a flat rock to reach
1.10 the **skiádi**, the mushroom ② (**P:** N 36°48.534'/ E 24°32.372'). A flat lump of rock lying on soft sandstone whose lower part has been sanded down by the wind in the course of time. This transient natural monument affords us shade for a brief respite.

!! For concentration is required from here on! Go right at a 90° angle to the track used up to now, down across white ledges of rock, past some cairns and towards a wide rock
!! ③. From there you follow the indistinct track, finally dropping down into the hollow at a wall. Architects are welcome to add to the cairns!

1.25 Shortly before you reach the dry stream-bed the path becomes more distinct again, leading through the **ditch** on the left and up to the monopáti which approaches from the right. It runs left to the sea, in the direction of Mílos, so we do not hesitate to join it ④. It is all plain sailing now. Just having to trample a few thorny companions underfoot, walking in the stream-bed, you eventually reach
2.00 the **Elliniká Bay**. Gravel – if you prefer something softer, amble left along the shore, looking out at the many rocks which seem to dance in the sea like elves.

Chóra – Elliniká Bay – Chóra   139

The rocky headland and the island beyond used to be connected. This is the site of the ancient town of Límni, which was abandoned during the Byzantine era.

Behind the rocky headland Dékas Bay offers the finest sand and tamarisks. Thanks to the shallow water, bathing temperatures are already inviting in spring. And we have certainly earned a dip. If you order a taxi in advance, you can extend the pleasure for even longer.

2.20 Sooner or later the more sporty among us have to get going and start walking along a dirt track running **inland** through a dune landscape. At the fork follow the ruts going right through gardens and fields, reaching the road on level ground.

Proceed left along the road for only 80 m – but without missing the rock garden with prickly pears and wine! At the right-hand bend in the road you turn left for 20 m un-
2.40 til you reach a **dirt track** on the right which, bordered by walls, runs along the coastline. Later it veers up left –
!! where you discover a mule track going *to the right.*

First running through a hollow, it then passes a sharp-
2.55 edged **chapel** (right). Disregard the turn-off to the right. After a hollow you walk uphill for quite a while until coming to a chapel (left) beside some barns and a water pond. From there you continue straight ahead and past another pond (left).

Gradually the houses rise up out of the hollow. After passing through a "suburb", you cross a bridge and return to
3.25 **Chóra**.

▶ **Accommodation:** Villa María (Chóra) 22870 513 92
Meltémi (Chóra)   22870 513 60
Sardi (Aliki Beach) 22870 514 58
Aliki   22870 513 40

Kíthnos

The relatively flat, rather barren island mainly consists of slate and limestone. On account of its hot springs it is a favourite destination of Greek health spa visitors. The island's proximity to Athens can lead to problems in finding accommodation at the weekends. But, apart from yachtsmen, international tourism passes Kíthnos by, which is precisely what makes this tranquil island so attractive.
Wonderful old footpaths still exist, accompanied by the typical north Cycladic dry-stone walls with vertically standing flat stone slabs. Shady trees are however an absolute rarity.

❸❽ 1537

In the fateful year 1537 almost all the Cycladic islands were occupied by the Turks. This five-hour trek along old tracks starts at the seaside resort of Loutrá and follows the traces of the Turkish conquerors right up to the ruin of the Venetian fortress Kastro Oriás (also Paléo Kástro). Unlike the warriors of those days we do not have to carry heavy gear with us, just food and water rations, for wholly trustworthy cisterns are in short supply. After all, we are rewarded with two very beautiful beaches and a coastal path, where we only have to climb over a few walls.
■ *11.5 km, difference in altitude 260 m, moderate*

AWT	Directly in front of the **hotel** "Porto Klaras" in **Loutrá** go
0.00	right up a couple of wide steps, past the chapel and left up the ramp after 15 m. Then on up steps and a track to the roadway, where you go left. Walking in an arc to the left
0.13	above Loutrá, you reach the **road**, where you go right.
0.15	After about 150 m  the trained eye finds the old **footpath** running down to the left opposite a ruin. The monopáti drops gently down into the valley, where you
0.20	soon come across reeds and a **cistern** by the wayside. 100 m further on you go left at the fork beside an olive tree and later, after the fig tree above the deeply carved in path (where a deep well lies concealed), you go left up the
0.30	**transversal monopáti**.
0.40	At the **junction** with a dirt track (**P:** N 37°27.416′/ E 24°25.066′) we also go left. The track, which can now be negotiated by robust vehicles, leads to a wide fork at the
0.45	top near the chapel of **Agios Fílippos**. Here we go left to the goat-sheds, where we soon pick out our destination for the day, the ruins of the fortress. Without a path you walk to the left of a wall, passing through a gateway,
0.55	and on up to the **rocky hill** beyond (**P:** N 37°27.748′/ E 24°24.763′). Here you have a magnificent view of the enormous lump of rock upon which stood the Venetian fortress **Kástro Oriás** .

At this very spot the Ottoman warriors lay in wait that night in the year 1537. The Venetians had dug a moat in front of the fortified town. It did not help against the ruse of war employed by the Turkish admiral Chaireddin Barbarossa: an expectant mother knocked on the gates and asked to be let in. As the gates opened, the sultan's warriors stormed the fortress. Only three out of the more than

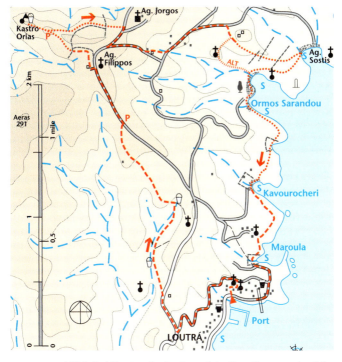

400 inhabitants who had sought refuge there survived the massacre alive.

Below the fortress on the left you pass through the gate decorated with crosses and easily find the path up to the
1.10 **Church of the Mother of God** (Kíra Eleoúsa) which was later built among the ruins. You will find a water tank here. Further down, between the destroyed houses, stands the vaulted Trinity church.

Slightly to the left of the hill in front of the fortress we set off back again, passing to the right of the next hill, above the former monastery of Agios Jórgos ③, and on to the
1.30 **dirt track**. There you bear right for a while, walking past the turn-off to the monastery as far as a fork 120 m ahead the Fílippos chapel. Now go 300 m left down the dirt
1.35 track until you come to a **ruined house** on the left. The somewhat concealed old monopáti branches off to the left here.

Loutrá – Paléokastro – Sóstis Beach – Loutrá   143

This monopáti is now only 100 m long. After that you must take the new dirt track, passing a few houses (right) and marching right down towards Agios Sóstis at the
1.45 fork. Down to the right is a tile-roofed chapel; on the hill to the left of it you can make out some ruined houses, our next destination. After a short march these ruins are on the right-hand side of the dirt track, from which you turn
1.50 off right on to a **mule track**.

Short cut: a second mule track leads to the right into the narrow valley below the tile-roofed chapel and on to Sarándou strand.

Having passed the dilapidated houses, head for the peninsula – not following any path and just surmounting two
2.05 walls –, where you go left to **Agios Sóstis strand** 4. Besides a chapel situated picturesquely on a ridge of land you will enjoy the pebble beach and wonderfully clear water. Sometimes moped cyclists like to use the new track. After relaxing here, we walk over the mountain ridge
2.15 without a path and come to the double bay of **Potámia Sarándou** with another chapel and shady tamarisks.

To reach the second bay behind the cliff, you have to follow a narrow path and climb down over a few rocks at the end of it. But running along the coastline on the flat from this bay are marvellous goat tracks which are easy to negotiate. Hiking trails commence at the walled-in field at
2.35 **Kavourochéri strand**. Shortly before Loutrá you pass beneath the old ore loading installations which have been rusting away for 60 years. We certainly haven't started to rust today, so proudly take a seat beneath a tamarisk in
3.00 **Loutrá** and let the waiter do the running for a change.

㊴ Old rivals

The only two villages in the interior of the island are Kíthnos and Driópis, also known as Chóra (island's central place) and Chórico (village). Each has always claimed to be the more important and beautiful place. Today we are going to decide for ourselves. Both villages used to be connected by a wide flagstone path, which has since had to make way for motorized traffic. However this trail, which is often recommended for hikers, is not the only pedestrian connection. The two-and-a-half hour trek described here also leads to the chóra, but the undergrowth is knee-high for about 50 m – a clear case for long trousers.
■ *6 km, difference in altitude 70 m, easy to moderate*

AWT **Driópis** (or Driopída, p.141) is easy to reach by bus. The village, whose appearance is almost Spanish, is hardly geared to tourism. Yet the beauty of the settlement and its surrounding topography is at least equal to that of the chóra.

0.00 From the **forecourt of the twin-towered church** you walk downhill for about 30 m and go straight down the steps beside the bakery (left). After 37 steps, above the valley, descend another 13 steps left to a concrete path. Wan-
0.05 der slowly down it, between the walls, to the green **valley bottom**.

Here you find a shady dirt track heading left – but only for two minutes! Now things start to get serious. Whitewashed steps ① lead up to the right and then, after ten

Driópis – Chóra 145

metres, on to the left at the fork. On the right above the valley you ascend, after a bend you see a chapel in a side valley and to the left of it our onward track in a saddle. Having traversed the floor of the side valley, we stroll

0.15 alongside gardens and a cistern (right) to a **fork** below the chapel (**P:** N 37°23.361'/ E 24°25.619').

Here we go left and on up the winding monopáti as far as the saddle (200 m) with a crossing of the ways, where

0.25 we go straight ahead. After 50 m we come to a **fork** (**P:** N 37°23.562'/ E 24°25.721') above a ruined house, from where we can see our destination behind a flat mountain ridge – the strung-out chóra, flanked by wind rotors.

At this fork you go right along the mule track, following the contour lines. On the left-hand side of the counter-slope you can make out two intermediate goals: a domed church and, to the left above it, on the next slope, another chapel. The path now descends into the valley and is covered with knee-high spherical spurge for about 50 m. Further down in a hollow you encounter thick oleander. Having started to go uphill again, on the right you pass the very old, three-aisled taxiarchis/archangel church ②, which was constructed with ancient columns and capitals and decorated with frescoes.

0.45 The monopáti ends beside a wayside altar at a **dirt track**, into which you turn left. This was the very old flagged kalderími which has been destroyed for the sake of the cars. However, if you go left at the fork which soon comes, you will still marvel at its elegant alignment on the way down to a stone bridge and a cistern, after which comes

0.55 the steep ascent to the **Trifou chapel**.

Now only one valley lies between us and the chóra. The former kalderími runs across this valley. Having passed

1.05 two **chapels** on the left of the path going uphill again, we
1.20 go over the hilltop and into the **chóra** of Kíthnos.

This village is much more geared to tourism than Driópis. The fabric-covered chairs of the inns are supposed to engender international flair. Yet the normal cane chairs, though rickety, would be just as fitting.

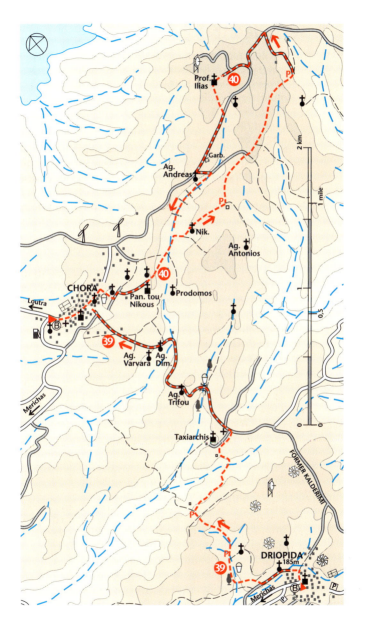

Dríopis – Chóra

40 Secluded trails

The four-hour hike leads from the chóra to the deserted monastery Profítis Elías on the island's highest peak, almost entirely along mule tracks. The monastery's charming courtyard affords welcome shade for a rest. The treeless region does however seem rather barren in autumn. Some low barriers have to be climbed over.
■ *9.5 km, difference in altitude 165 m, moderate*

▷ Map see previous page

AWT 0.00 — From the **bus stop in Chóra** you go down the one-way street, past the monument (right), straight ahead, along the rows of café-chairs on the main street. After passing the domed church with the bell hanging outside (right), you go through the house-bridge over the alleyway.

Five metres later you turn off right and descend some steps as far as a house, where you turn left. Proceeding almost horizontally, you now go past a chapel (right) into a long alley, at the end of which, on the edge of the village,

0.05 stands a **well** on the left. Going down to the right there, you come to a monopáti, past a cistern in the hollow and to a chapel outside the village.

Here you continue left, then, at the fork in the concrete path after 80 m, up to the right. On your left the wind rotors of a German-Greek project stand – often idle. The trail takes a further left-hand bend, leading to the large

0.15 **Panagía tous Nikous monastery** 1. The French window affords a glimpse of the church's beautiful interior. The

148 Kíthnos

ancient structural parts lying around are a reminder of the long history of this place.

To the left of the church a very fine mule track leads on along the right-hand side of the mountain, later dropping into a hollow. On the mountain in the direction of movement you can already pick out the white dots of the Elias monastery.

0.20 A few metres above the next hollow is a **fork**, where you go down left and left again in the dry stream-bed. After 40 m the path forks again – leave the stream-bed up to the right. (You will come past this point on the return leg.)

Having gone up left at a further fork and passed the Nikoláos chapel (right) ②, you head on along a ridgeway
0.30 as far as a major **fork** with house ruins on the right (**P:** N 37°24.639'/ E 24°26.935').

From here you make for Profítis Elías, so turn left ③. On the right you see the rugged east coast, on the left, less uplifting, the rubbish tip.

0.35 Cross a **dirt track**, then – after four minutes – ignore the monopáti's right-hand turn-off. The Elias monastery lies behind the hill on your left and cannot be seen from here. Above the small valley with a tile-roofed chapel you continue climbing gently. Below some farmhouses you climb over a low wooden barrier, soon arriving at the gateway to
0.50 a **dirt track** (**P:** N 37°24.830'/ E 24°27.635').

This is where we leave our monopáti, which heads right into the valley, and ascend steeply to the left, with the farmstead on our left. After a level stretch the dirt track
1.00 comes to a wider sand track at a **sliding gate**, where we go left. Now you cannot miss our destination ④. Go right up the dirt track at a gate into some grass land. This is

Chóra – Profítis Elías – Chóra   149

	however not the real path; further on you therefore have to scale a wall to reach the **Profítis Elías monastery**. Apart from the newly laid stairway everything is very agreeable to the eye. Time for a rest in the shade of the monastery walls.
1.10	

however not the real path; further on you therefore have

1.10 to scale a wall to reach the **Profítis Elías monastery**. Apart from the newly laid stairway everything is very agreeable to the eye. Time for a rest in the shade of the monastery walls.

To return, we use the correct path: through the covered passageway, past the benchmark on the right, along the

1.15 wall to the **road** and on downhill. Just past the rubbish tip is the way to the Andreas chapel.

> *Alternative:* continuing along the sand track would be less strenuous, as you do not have to negotiate any barriers (see below). But it is not as pleasant.

At the Andreas chapel you stroll left along the dirt track

1.30 into the **hollow** and, right on or beside the path, in the stream-bed. In the direction of movement you see the monastery Panagía tous Nikous again. Having skipped over about four low barriers, you return to the place beneath the Nicolas chapel.

Pay no attention to the left-hand turn-off this time. Go

1.40 right at the next **fork** (= AWT 0.20 on outward route), up
1.45 left 50 m further. Striding past **Our Lady's Monastery**,
1.55 you quickly reach **Chóra**. It now being siesta time, though, you may have to search until you find any refreshments!

Island hopping

Journeys through the Greek islands are among the most beautiful and relaxing travel experiences, for thanks to connecting boat services it is possible to let yourself drift across the sea. The bustle which accompanies docking and casting off, the greeting and leave-taking in each port are a special experience with almost all of the island's inhabitants taking part.

Yet this type of travel is sometimes accompanied by an element of chance. Strong winds, especially in August, can easily shake up the timetable. Hence you should not be set on trying to catch the last boat on the day before your flight home.

Mílos

The flat mining island lies on the south Aegean seismic arc (see page 10). It was built up gradually in layers formed by volcanoes. One of the volcanoes is still active today, albeit on a small scale. The Bay of Mílos is not a caldera, however, having been formed by displacement. The natural beauty-spots of this rather barren island face the sea: here one can walk and bathe along the spectacular rocky coastline. One such possibility is described in walk 41. The mining industry has led to massive intrusions into the natural landscape – that is why one almost only finds dirt roads in the eastern part of the island. More suitable for hiking is the lonely, yet hardly accessible western half below the Profítis Elías. Mílos also makes a good starting point for walks on the island of Kímolos.

🟠 Dream coast

This four to five-hour hike leads along the north coast without paths. You can walk in shorts and sandals with good soles. The beaches have no tavernas and are partly deserted.
The second part of the trek leads through wonderful rock formations.
■ *9 km, difference in altitude 70 m, easy*

Take the Pollónia bus to Fylakopí.
Fylakopí was the first capital of the island and the centre of the obsidian trade with the whole Mediterranean region.

Mílos 151

Excavations have unearthed four towns built on top of each other, dating from between 2300 and 1100 BC. The frescoes discovered have now been moved to the National Museum in Athens. On site it is still possible to make out a huge defence wall of cyclopean stonework and the ground plan of interlocking houses.

AWT 0.00 The trek begins at the **bus stop in Fylakopí**. (If you intend to terminate your hike in Mytakas, the return times of the buses are listed here). It is easy to find the rocky path between the road and the sea which leads you to the first bay between the cliffs in three minutes. Having gone over a bridge of rock, then directly above the water, you

0.10 arrive in the holiday resort of **Papáfraga**. Take the dirt track here up right towards the sea and then bear left to the sandy bay. A dirt track behind it leads up on to a sort of heath and then back down towards the rocky shore. Seagulls from the island of Glaronissiá vis-à-vis do low-flying exercises here in the spring. At the end of the rugged,

0.25 scree landscape is the small **barrel-roofed church** of Agios Konstantínos. Not until you get closer do you see the hidden small fishermen's houses and the harbour 1. The rock in the sea ahead forms a double-spanned bridge 2. After the church wall we turn off right, then immediately left, walking over solidified lava above a huge grotto, which is not recognizable as such until later. After the large sandy bay follows another smaller bay on the right. Now it is possible to walk right out along the spit, before carrying on over the flat rock directly at the water's edge. Having broken away and now been separated from the mainland by a five-metre stretch of water, a large rock is occupied by raucous seagulls in the spring. We jump over

long, narrow crevices in which the water bubbles. This unreal landscape ③ was created by the rock being compacted under repeated pressure. The remaining vegetation has been forced to the ground by the wind. The rock pools are large enough to take a refreshing bathe. The na-
0.50 tural harbour of **Mytakas**, with its picturesque small houses, lies at the bend in the coastline.

Short cut: on the road above you can reach the bus stop in five minutes. Mind you, the most beautiful rocks are still to come!

Having passed the harbour, we reach a wide sandy bay with two tamarisks and two hewn grottos. Above this be-
★ gins the wondrous world of the **Sarakíniko Coast**. It consists of sandstone and limestone, eroded and polished into bizarre shapes by wind and water. It is undoubtedly one of the most beautiful coastlines in Europe ④. Flat rocks lie in the water; the steep cliffs rising up from the sea sometimes take on the appearance of a herd of elephants at a watering place. Wandering above the cliffs, you
1.25 feel as if you were among desert dunes. A **road** appears from further up, bringing numerous visitors down. They also find a kiosk in the cleft.

Alternative: the sporty among us can wander on over the green crest of the next headland, arriving in the picturesque fishing village of **Mantrákia** in 15 minutes. From there, however, you have another 25 minutes before reaching the bus station in Péra Triovássalos.

Fylakopí – Sarakíniko Coast – Adámas

Pleasure-seekers remain on the Sarakíniko Coast for a while, enjoying the rounded rock formations. When our eyes are sated, we put our shoes back on, walk up the road to the main road in about twelve minutes, then turn right along it for 100 m before heading to the left near the power pole and over the ridge without a path. The huge Bay of Mílos, Ormos Miloy, is visible below and we find paths and tracks over some fairly unremarkable terrain down to

2.00 **Adámas**.

A short trek for pleasure-seekers:
Anyone who just wants to see the Sarakíniko Coast, preferring to spend more time swimming and sunbathing, should take the bus only as far as the **Mykátas fork**, walk five minutes down to the harbour (AWT 0.50 of the main trek) and stroll on left from there.

▶ The Brau Kat travel agency located in Adámas harbour specializes in gentle tourism and frequently organizes walks for small groups, including on the otherwise hardly accessible and uninhabited neighbouring island of **Poliégos**.

🟠 The last volcano

In the south-east of the island is the large extinct volcano Tsigrádo, which lies mostly beneath the sea. The part on land forms an extensive round crater with tilled fields.
The five-hour circular tour starting from Zerifíria takes you along dirt tracks and narrow trails to the crater, where you can smell the bad breath from the bowels of the earth. Before that you pass through a landscape which is quite untypical of the islands. Currently there is nowhere to stop along the way.
■ *11 km, difference in altitude 120 m, moderate*

AWT Unless you want to use the school bus at some unearthly hour, you have to take a taxi or hire a moped to get to **Zefiría**, which, with 5000 inhabitants, was the island's main town until 1750.

Following an earthquake in Santoríni the earth emitted sulphurous vapours here which contaminated the air and the soil. When diseases broke out, the town was abandoned between 1720 and 1767. The more than 400-year-old church Panagía Portianí, the island's former episcopal church, lay in ruins for a long time and was only rebuilt 100 years ago. It has been almost completely painted again. Today 200 people still live here and fewer people live on the whole of Mílos than used to live in Zefiría alone.

0.00 From the church walk back to the **fork** and left along the road at the sign "Paliochório". Already after 150 m, though, you turn right at the 30 km sign on to a dirt track

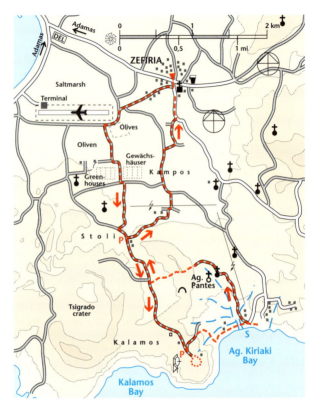

which is lined by extra-wide walls. In the direction of sight and movement you see the mighty Profítis Elías; on the left tower the edges of the crater. It is only possible to discern the outlines of the cutaway entrance.

0.10 The trail approaches the **airport**, on the perimeter of which you turn left, then go round the corner and along the fence (right) for 120 m. At the edge of the wall surrounding an olive grove (left) you turn off to the left. In the direction of movement you see greenhouses. This region is called Kámpos and is the island's granary. The fertile volcanic soil is used to cultivate not just corn, but potatoes, tomatoes, grapes and vegetables. Straightforward, unspectacular farming country.

0.20 At a fork you go left to the **greenhouses**. At the green

156   **Mílos**

"traffic island" beyond them you turn left and immediately afterwards right again, thus continuing in the same direction. You pass a strange building topped by a large concrete frame.

Having passed the fields, you come to a heath and turn right at the first fork and then left at the following triangular "traffic island". Fields have been laid out at the very edge of the crater, higher up is scrub. In this area,

0.35 called "**Stóli**", stands another of these strange buildings and right beside it a pump room (**P:** N 36°40.988'/ E 24°28.926').

A narrow valley leads into the former crater. It is covered with cornfields which form a bizarre contrast with the

0.45 dark green cedars ①. At a **right-hand bend** you march briskly straight ahead until you come to the red-tinged rocky ledge overlooking the sea. Below to the left you see the coastal plain of Agios Kiriakí ②, with Folégandros in the background; up on the right stands an antenna. The

1.00 dirt track finishes at a fairly large **building** (**P:** N 36° 40.109'/ E 24°25.462'). The region is called "Kálamos".

We are drawn towards the red cliffs. First go left, but veer right into an area surrounded by rocks 80 m before a barn. Everywhere the earth's crust emits hissing sulphurous vapours. Walk across the eerily beautiful spot in a clockwise direction, where you will even find a tunnel, and re-

1.20 turn to the large **building**.

There tracks branch off to the right, which you follow

!! downhill. But in the *second bend to the left*, after approx. three minutes, you go *straight ahead* and leave the dirt track. A track leads between two prominent bushes towards the coastal plain. Then you continue downhill on the boundary between field and scrub. After a fence you go through some rocks – bearing right. Markings help you down the not very steep descent.

1.35 Down at the **shore**, around the houses, you can only evade the glorious muddle of usable and unusable objects by looking out to sea. Further north a fine sandy beach with tamarisks compensates for the visual intrusions. Maybe someone will re-open the deserted kiosk.

Retrace your steps from the strand, going up a concrete road in the direction of "Agios Pantes" at the first house on the right. On your right you see narrow eroded ravines with almost vertical pumice stone walls.

Plodding sternly on up through the grey region, the
1.50 **Pántes chapel** (left) and the ruins of its predecessor
chapel on the opposite side of the ravine provide a welcome diversion. From there you proceed through unusu-
al, undulating layers of rock as far as the edge of the
crater.

2.00 From **up** here you again see the large fields inside the
crater. First to the left, then to the right of the fence you
make your way down to the already familiar trail. Walk
2.05 back along the **dirt track** to the **pump rooms of Stolí**
2.20 (**P:** see above) and then turn right at the crossroads. Now
you roam over field and meadow, heading for the white
domes of the church in Zefiría, which from a distance
looks more like a mosque.

2.25 Go left at the **fork**, at the next fork beneath the power
line likewise, and continue towards the village. Go
2.30 straight ahead at the **junction** where a track joins from
the right, the greenhouses far away to the left. The hills
surrounding the plain bear witness to the ubiquity of the
local mining industry. Rock has been quarried everywhere, leaving open wounds in the natural landscape.
"Recultivation" is one of the few words which is not of
Greek origin.

Approaching the village you turn off to the right at the
signpost "Ag. Kiraki", then immediately afterwards left at
2.50 the next one. Walk left along the road into **Zefiría**.

▶ Taxi tel.: 2 28 02 22 19

158   **Mílos**

43 A long history

A four-hour trek from Adámas to the most important historic sites and places of cultural interest on the island. It is advisable to wear long trousers – not just because of the sacred places, but also to protect your legs! Large stretches lead without a path above the sea, offering a magnificent view of the bay. Finding your way is easy, but a degree of sure-footedness is required. However it is possible to avoid the difficult passages. Klíma has a place to stop. In low season the catacombs are only open until 1 pm!
■ *6 km, difference in altitude 170 m, moderate to difficult*

AWT 0.00 Behind the **jetty** in **Adámas**, in a cave on the right, are public hot springs such as were found all over the island in earlier times. We follow the shore path north to the hotels in Lagáda bay.

Alternative: The route described here leads across open terrain, climbing gently without a path for 25 minutes. If you wish to avoid this, take the asphalt road to the right behind the hotels and later the second turn-off up left. Further on a dirt track goes off to the left and on a left-hand bend round a hill and past the antenna to AWT 0.40. This variant has no sea views to offer, though.

The more interesting route leads directly along the edge of the water and on over a hilltop to the next, more peaceful bay. Here we come across a graveyard and a monument from 1897. It was set up in memory of the French-

Adámas – Klíma – Pláka   159

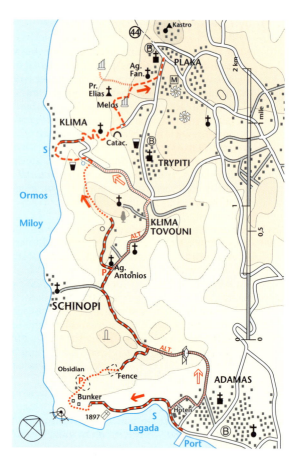

men who died of the plague here in the harbour, aboard the ships of the expedition corps during the Crimean War (1853–56). French influences were felt on Mílos from 1800. French soldiers also found their final resting-place here during the First World War.

The vast natural harbour, one of the largest in the Mediterranean, has always been of great strategic importance and was the cause of the repeated conquests of the island through the ages.

Behind the monument the trail soon ends and we head

0.15   uphill to the **beacon** without a path. Behind it are traces of the island's most recent history. The builders came from Germany, as can be deciphered on the blasted concrete of the bunkers from 1943.

Up to the left you see a rocky hilltop with a white marker post. Heading diagonally in this northerly direction to a shed on the next plateau, you arrive at a huge Stone Age weapons workshop (**P:** N 36°43.363′/ E 24°25.956′). Here, below a fence, black **obsidian**, a compact glassy rock which forms a crust on lava streams, was split and made into tools and weapons. Mílos was one of the earliest Cycladic islands to be inhabited, with traces going back as far as the 3rd millennium BC.

Continuing over the black rock, as though walking on coals ①, we head for the marker post. On the topmost

0.30   plateau is a **fenced-in area**. Going round it, you find
0.40   tracks on the other side leading inland to the **dirt track** which could have been used to get here (see above).

Now go left, past a shed (right), bearing right at a fork and walk towards Tripití, which shines down from above.

0.45   Soon you reach the **rural chapel** of Saint Antonius, which stands protecting the olive tree next to it ②. (**P:** N 36°43.389′/ E 24°25.944′).

> *Alternative:* the second half of the following route to Klíma is pathless, partly leading through scrub. You can avoid it by continuing straight ahead and then descending left along the road to Klíma.
>
> This option has no sea views to offer, unless you care to make a detour to the chapel of Klimatovoúni.

0.45   In front of the Antonious chapel a wall-lined dirt track bears left. Running near a farmhouse, it leads between vegetable fields above the sea and on to picture-book
0.50   **olive tree terraces** ③. On the other side of the huge bay towers the mountain of the Prophet and down below the
★   ferries bring in holidaymakers, the new conquerors of the island.

Having torn yourself away from the beautiful view, you climb down five metres and follow the terrace, along which a mule track leads further north. Where the terraces end, you have to climb over low walls and should then keep uphill rather than downhill. The terraces continue here too, though they are now covered with scrub. Soon you catch sight of the fishing village of Klíma below.

Adámas – Klíma – Pláka   161

When going down through the phrýgana, it is advisable to keep right on the mountain as the slopes drop away steeply! Above the houses the track becomes even steeper, before you reach the road at **Klíma**. Next to the restaurant "Panorama" you climb down a narrow path to the picturesque **harbour**, where shady benches wait beneath the tamarisks.

Proceed 300 m into the gorge until, up to the left, you see the highlight of the trek: the remains of the immense wall of the ancient town of Melos. To get up there, climb the white-painted steps which ascend to the left of the road, past a church in a grotto. At the top of the steps walk a few metres along a level track and then left over pumice up to the **catacomb** ticket office.

This underground cemetery, the largest in Greece, was secretly laid out by the Christian community in the 3rd century AD. 7000 to 8000 dead lie buried here. The first 30 m of the system of chambers are open to visitors. In low season they are closed on Mondays.

We continue 120 m up along the track, turning off left on to a footpath before the next cave. Soon looming on the right are the cyclopean walls of the Dorian fortifications. You are standing on the site of **Old Melos** and shortly afterwards you reach the Roman amphitheatre.

The city was inhabited from 1000 BC to 1000 AD. It was founded by the Dorians, who had previously destroyed Fylakopí. Later the Romans also erected buildings on the site, including the still well preserved theatre with its superb position [4]. What an experience it must have been to watch a play being performed against this natural backdrop!

Continue straight on for a while and then up to the right.

1.35 Above the theatre is a round vehicle **turning area**. (If you take the dirt track to the right, you come to the place where the "Venus" now on display in the Louvre was found).

From here your route leads left on a dirt track through the hollow below the summit chapel and later right to a kalderími leading uphill.

Alternatives: on the left a partially overgrown track leads to the summit chapel of Profítis Elías where, in Roman times, an Apollo temple used to stand.

At a fork below this chapel it is possible to go right, down to the place where Roman villas were found. After eight minutes you come to a few columns on the left. Significant floor mosaics were discovered here, but they had to be covered up again as a means of protection. "Unassailable dream position", as the real estate brochure would put it nowadays.

1.45 The kalderími reaches the top of **Pláka** in a transversal alley. Go left up some steps, left again at the following alley, left yet again immediately afterwards and then straight ahead on the flat. Having passed *Betty's Studios* (left), you walk left uphill at the fork, then right. To be absolutely sure, though, it is advisable to ask for the **Panagía Kor-**

1.50 **fiatíssa** ("the" sunset rendezvous) or the **bus station** ("leoforío").

If you proceed straight on from there and continue to the right for another 15 minutes at the fork, you come to the **kástro**. The Venetians ruled the island from this fortress from 1207 until 1566.

A perfect way to end a day steeped in history or, for the sake of it, you can visit the very well appointed museum (closed Mondays).

Hikers with stamina could end up by joining ㊹.

44 Sunset

The most famous place to enjoy the sunset is of course the wall in front of Panagía Korfiatíssa church in Pláka. Those keen to experience the spectacle alone, however, should undertake this two-hour circular trek and not forget to take their bathing-trunks either.

■ *4.5 km, difference in altitude 170 m, easy*

AWT 0.00 — From the **bus station in Pláka** (near Panagía church) you go north-west along the wide alley, which divides after a few metres. A sign points right up to the kástro.

If you go *down left*, you immediately find a kalderími leading out of this beautiful town. Soon a path – which is admittedly overgrown further down – descends left to the small fishing village of Aretí. On the right-hand side of the

0.05 path you notice **whitewashed steps**, which indicate a path going right (see short cut below). We continue straight on downhill, cross a dirt track and are not at all pleased that from here on the old footpath has been replaced by a dirt track.

0.10 At the next **turn-off** (with power line) you go left for 30 m. In front of the sharp-angled garden wall of a holiday complex you turn off right and saunter down a kalderími to

0.15 the fishing village of **Fourkovoúni** ①. You follow the dirt track up to the right. At the next fork you head down for

0.25 the white **sandy beach of Pláthienas**, where you might find an open cantina. If this spot is really to your liking, you can celebrate the sunset here and arrange to be picked up by a taxi.

164 Mílos

Short cut: The track described below runs through thick undergrowth for about 120 m. So for the return leg you could take the already familiar trail, circumnavigating Fourkovoúni and, further up at the white steps at AWT 0.05, take a path which runs left to St. George's chapel (AWT 0.55).

0.25 Otherwise you march on up the asphalt road from the **beach** and, after the first left-hand bend, turn off at the second right-hand turn-off. Having taken a dirt track across the valley bottom, you walk up to an olive grove.

Proceeding right through the grove and across the terraces, you climb over a low field wall. Keeping immediately to the right of this wall, you now make your way up through the undergrowth without a path in the direction of the prominent rock. Above the grove you continue ascending in the same direction beside an overgrown monopáti. Below the prominent rock you later come

0.45 across a well-beaten **track**, where you go left. Beside a barn (right) you find a dirt track, which you follow left to the

0.50 **road**, but leave this again at once by joining a dirt track on the right.

Gradually climbing up this rather overgrown track, you have the vertiginous wooden balconies of two houses hanging above you on the kástro hill on the left and a distant view of the sea, dominated by the island of Antimílos, on the right.

At a sort of fork you proceed left up to the cave chapel

0.55 **Agios Geórgios** ②. Inside it is half natural, half man-made. In front of it lies the small resting place for that private sunset we were promised ...

In front of this spot is a track which will bring you back to

1.00 the already familiar kalderími and up left to **Pláka**, where the crowd of sun-worshipers has now disappeared.

Pláka – Pláthienas Beach – Pláka   165

Sérifos

Sérifos is relatively mountainous and sometimes appears to be barren, its name meaning "infertile". Stretching across the middle of the island is an elongated massif consisting of granite and gneiss, where the highest peak, Troúlos, reaches the formidable height of 582 m. The western side drops more steeply down to the sea than the eastern side, where the chóra built half way up the mountain looks down on pleasantly green slopes and beautiful sandy beaches.
On summer weekends many Athenians come and occupy the hotel beds in Livádi. Otherwise the island is not overrun, being just the place for hikers in search of tranquillity. In the mountainous hinterland it still offers a few old and now marked tracks, numerous wells and one of the most exciting kalderími on the Cyclades (see left). Walks ㊻ and ㊼ are specially recommended.

㊺ Above the chóra

This four-hour hike, one of the finest on the Cyclades, leads along a narrow track into fertile high-lying valleys and back to the chóra of Sérifos via one of the most superb paved paths.
Although the track uphill is partly rather unclear, orientation is not a problem. There are no wells along the route and no kafenía until you get back to Chóra.
■ *8 km, difference in altitude 460 m, moderate to difficult.*

▷ *Map see page 170*

AWT
0.00

In Livádi you walk inland from the bus stop, past the bakeries and up to the left soon afterwards. Having passed the sports field and the telephone box (right), turn right below a hotel and walk straight ahead, keeping on the same level the whole time. You pass the hotel "Panorama",

Livádi – Chóra   167

with the commercial zone below and Chóra above. Our first destination is the cruciform-domed basilica of Agía Ekateríni at the end of the valley.

After a carpenter's shop you turn right and, at a sharp right-hand bend in the sand road, left. At the concrete silos you go down to a chicken-coop, immediately left beside the house and then, for about 50 m, to the left of a eucalyptus tree, through a hollow without a path. Next to a low wall on the other side you find a small path which continues more or less in the same direction as up to now. Later, down on the right, a monopáti leads to the road.

0.25 In front of St. Catharine's church 1 you cross the **streambed** and walk left upstream on the other side. Having gone across a small valley which joins from the right, you
0.30 are confronted by the **sharp-cornered wall** of a garden with a small house. Continue to the right of it, after a few metres turning up to the right into a small side valley. On the left are brambles, on the right walls. Having changed to the other side of the valley by clearing a way through the brambles, you meet, below some ruins, the transversal main route which leads right to Chóra. We go left there
0.35 and soon come through a **rocky wind-gap**.

From here on the trail is rather unclear. Bear right after the wind-gap, keeping 10–30 m to the right of the *black*
!! *water pipe*. It will accompany us for over half an hour and facilitate orientation. Later you go immediately to the right of it and come past the flat-roofed **St. John's chapel**. Then you walk to the left of the pipe, even though it temporarily disappears from view. Cross the rocks on narrow tracks.

Rising up out of the sea like the top of a mast you first no-

168   Sérifos

0.55 tice the white bell tower, then **Panagía Chapel** (**P:** N 37°09.137'/ E 24°29.317'). Seated at the masonry table you look across to Chóra while preparing a small picnic. On the other side of the slope you discover the remains of a track leading up to Mount Kefála.

Behind the chapel, to the left of the reeds, you climb uphill ②, where you run into the black pipe again beside a small house. On the counterslope on the left stands another chapel, beside it on the left are antennae. Below a one-roomed house we leave our trusty companion, the pipe, and, bearing right, soon come to several houses (right) and a dirt track.

1.15 Walk left along this and then up to the right at the **fork** (**P:** N 37°09.361'/ E 24°28.385', 385 m). The hiker is surrounded by spacious, gently rolling and fertile countryside. The dirt track runs past a long water collection basin (left) before coming to a turn-off to the left. Here we climb up to the *right* past a dilapilated barn (right) in the direction

1.25 of the orange-coloured flag of the **helicopter pad**, which we soon pass on the right.

Spread out below on the opposite side of the high-lying valley stands a solitary chapel, our next destination. The trail leading there is marked "2" on the red-and-white me-

1.35 tal signs. From the **St. George's chapel** you have one of
★   the most exciting panoramas on the Cyclades: a bird's eye view of the chóra of Sérifos, behind that the small island Vous. Then you have the pleasure of taking one of the most beautiful kalderími which you will find anywhere nowadays (p. 166). It was laboriously constructed to connect the ore mines around Méga Livádi with Chóra. It is only when strolling down it that one appreciates the builders' colossal achievement, happily pausing for a mi-

1.55 nute's silence before proceeding into **Chóra**.

Livádi – Chóra   169

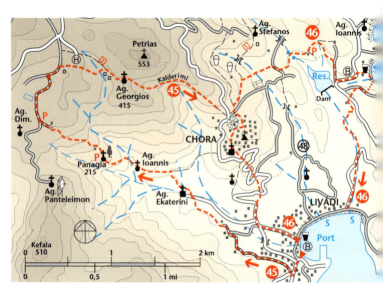

㊻ Below the chóra

This three-and-a-half hour trek leads along the old paved path up to chóra. After your visit the route takes you on over the other side through undulating, fertile countryside and down to the sand-dunes of Psilí Ammos.

■ *7.5 km, difference in altitude 220 m, moderate*

AWT	
0.00	The trek begins at the **pedestrian bridge** directly on Livádi strand. You go up the road, turn right at the large bridge and go right off the road after 200 m. On the out-
0.30	skirts of the village you pass a **domed church**, from where you continue up to the right. Using the road for 50 m, you then take the stepped path on the right again. At the
0.40	forks below the rock, bear left to the attractive **platía**.
	To the right of the town hall a small lane ① leads downhill and left after 60 m. Ahead of the bus stop beside the kafeníon "Myloi" turn down right on to the track which
0.45	leads out of Chóra. Having passed a **group of houses**, do not go down the dirt track on the right after 50 m, but

170   Sérifos

	proceed straight ahead for a further 250 m, then down right at the power poles and through a green valley. As you climb, the cemetery remains on your right. Further
0.55	up on the left is a **dovecote**. Shortly after that you cross a dirt track, yet continue walking, now a little further to the right, on the mule track, which leads between boulders
1.00	and into a rocky **valley floor**.

Water-holes have been carved into the granite. After encouraging the frogs there to break a few records in the long jump, we contentedly continue on up the path, which hugs the side of the slope and leads left up the val-

1.05 ley. At a small **house** (right) (**P:** N 37°09.768′/ E 24°30.910′) we go straight on along a wall-lined monopáti.

In a hollow the accompanying walls spread out until they are 15 m apart. Directly beside the right-hand wall you go
!! uphill and, half way up, turn off to *the right* on to a path.
1.10 This path brings you to a **dirt track** running downhill and, after a few holiday houses (left), to the left of the
1.15 new reservoir, to the **road**.

Proceed left along this down the hill, finally using the
1.20 steps down to the sandy beach of **Psilí Ammos** 2. Besides fine sand it offers tamarisks and two tavernas. Should you care to linger longer here, there is always the bus stop at the top of the steps ...

If you prefer to go on foot, work your way up from the southern end of the bay without a path to a dirt track run-
1.30 ning along the slope above the bay; this leads to the **road**. On the other side of the road a path runs down into the broad valley below the reservoir, from where it continues
1.50 back to **Livádi**.

Livádi – Chóra – Psili Ammos – Livádi   171

㊼ The monastery of the archangels

The most famous sight on Sérifos is the Moní ton Taxiarchón, a more than 400-year old fortified monastery. It is still possible to make the long trek there on an old pilgrims' path, but you need to be fit and have seven to eight hours to spare. So you should do like the pilgrims and rise early. Along the way are plenty of springs, but no tavernas – quite in keeping with the route's religious nature.
■ *14 km, difference in altitude 205 m, difficult*

AWT 0.00 — Not quite like the pilgrims we catch a **bus to Chóra**. After stocking up with edibles beside the bus stop, set off to the left of kafeníon ΜΥΛΟΙ, "Mills", down a few steps, right on the concrete path and then immediately left down the hill. A paved path leads to a group of houses and then out

0.05 — into the open countryside. At the **first fork** you go straight ahead, and again at the next one. Head for the mountains which are "crowned" by two antennae.

0.10 — The trail drops into a hollow with an old **stone bridge** ①, beside which the first well is waiting. Sérifos is proud of its allegedly one hundred wells and today we can test a few of them. Climb up from the bridge, following the local red-and-white path marked "1". On the crest of the hill is a house beside St. Stephen's chapel (right). On the other side of the dirt track you go into the next valley and on to

0.20 — the next **bridge**. Not nearly as elegant as the first one, yet unmistakable on account of its *curved steel railings*.

!! — Then you walk along a sunken track. When the lateral walls come to an end, you should watch out: the track

172 Sérifos

forks here imperceptibly! (**P:** N 37°10.111'/ E 24°30.402')
Go left, following the "metallic one" (㊽ leads to the right).

Passing some ruins (left), you come up to the flat-roofed
0.35 **Páno Stavrós chapel** with blue bell-tower ②. As the name suggests, this is the "upper" holy-cross chapel as well as being a crossroads. It is pleasantly cool inside, even providing a small table for a little rest, that one is in absolutely no hurry to leave the semi-darkness again.

The trail becomes wider from here on, a clear indication of the number of pilgrims who must have used it. Hugging the edge of the hill, you can refresh your geography of the Cyclades: Sífnos, Kímolos, Mílos – from left or
0.50 right? The skilfully laid kalderími leads past a **pen** (right) before becoming a gravel track. Pity about the destruction of a rural cultural asset.

From the saddle (355 m) you look down upon Kéndarchos, according to the islanders the prettiest village. That is why it is also called kallítsos, "the most beautiful one". Follow the track down to the new road. Go left along it for about 100 m, then right down the steps and left into **Kén-**
1.05 **darchos**. It only has a few alleyways, in the main alley is a well with cool spring water; the inhabitants seldom put in an appearance.

From the well the main alley leads uphill and through the adjacent, abandoned hamlet Kámpos. After hut no. 117
1.15 do not go left to the road, but *straight ahead* to a **monopáti**. Where its walls widen out, you go down to the right for a few metres, but left again alongside a wall as soon as the concrete surface finishes. On your right out to sea lies Kíthnos, in the foreground appears quite a large new church.

At an electricity meter go left up the road leading to the church and find a mule track on the right after 80 m. It runs parallel to the road for a while, later ending at an **oak grove**. Take the monopáti which crosses there, go right down it for 20 m and then first left. Maintaining your original direction, you follow the contour lines. Further on the monopáti no longer has a wall on the right.

Where power lines lead downhill, you cross a low field
1.35 wall and come up to the **road** on a dirt track. You can now
1.50 catch up on lost time, quickly reaching **Taxiarchón Monastery** (230 m) ③.

Chóra – Kéndarchos – Moní Taxiarchión – Galaní – Chóra

Monk Makários (page 3) takes cares of the surrounding communities from here. The tiny portal to the monastery, which used only to be accessible via a ladder, protected a machicolation. The 10 m high fortified monastery dates from the 15th century and has 60 rooms, which are picturesquely grouped round the church. It used to accommodate 30 monks and 30 lay brethren. In the church of the Saints Michael and Gabriel Makários proudly shows the dazzling altar screen made of marble and the gold-plated wood carving with a wonderful icon by the famous artist Skordilis.

The road veers left to the bus stop (departure approx. 3.30 pm). Concrete steps lead downhill; this is trekking route "6" according to the local signs. Soon you arrive in **Galaní** ("the sky-blue one"), a sloping village in the centre of which stands a church with a modern concrete cross. The inhabitants used to earn a living from keeping silkworms. You may be lucky and find a kafeníon that is open.

Walking horizontally in a curve to the left, you cross the village and come to the access road on the other side. Go up this for about 120 m and then turn right on to narrow
2.05 **path**. Route "6" leads you along the edge of the slope, above the valley bottom on your right. In the hollow with thick oleander bushes you cross a concrete bridge and then the beautiful, narrow path starts to ascend again.
2.10 Where it forks, head right up to a **dirt track**.

30 m further to the left, you again go uphill, past Polikarpos chapel (left) and a farmhouse with a water tap in the garden. The two friendly occupants are glad to see visitors. From there steps made of lumps of rock lead further uphill, before forking *to the right*. In the saddle you pass

174 **Sérifos**

2.35 the Sotiras-Chapel ④, where you turn off to the left and continue on up the fall line to the **road**.

Across the road are concrete steps which bring you through the deserted hamlet **Pírgos** ("tower"). 20 m below the chapel turn left and walk down a monopáti to a large well on the road.

A welcome pit stop before the final ascent of the day, which starts right behind the well. Once more giving of your best, you quickly gain height by going zig-zag through the boulders and are able to proudly look down at Galaní. The going gets easier at the top. Without a path, walking immediately to the right of a fence, you proceed up to altitude 435 according to the map. Where the fence takes a sharp bend, we follow it to the left as far as an uncontrolled rubbish tip (right) where, below the

2.55 antennae, we come to a **dirt track**.

The descent can commence: first right on the wide dirt track, then straight ahead where the track takes a right-hand bend. After that you go down to the right of a vineyard in the direction of Chóra. The trail swings to the right and veers past a tallish house, before becoming a rather overgrown monopáti, where you can sometimes see the thick white cobwebs left by the silkworms.

Further down the trail more or less peters out, so you continue into the valley without a path and head for the following point: on the counterslope across the valley, on the left below a cube-shaped Constantine chapel, you will notice a monopáti leading down to the area below where you are standing – that is where to make for!

In no time at all you reach this green and proliferous area

3.20 at the **bottom of the valley** and so can take it easy on the

3.35 final stretch on up towards Chóra. Having crossed a **dirt track** on a slant to the left, you are rewarded with a fa-

★ bulous view of Chóra. Lost in reverie, you wander between the terraces, traverse a trough with a well and arrive

3.50 in **Chóra**. Phew, we have certainly earned a drink now, but no water please this time.

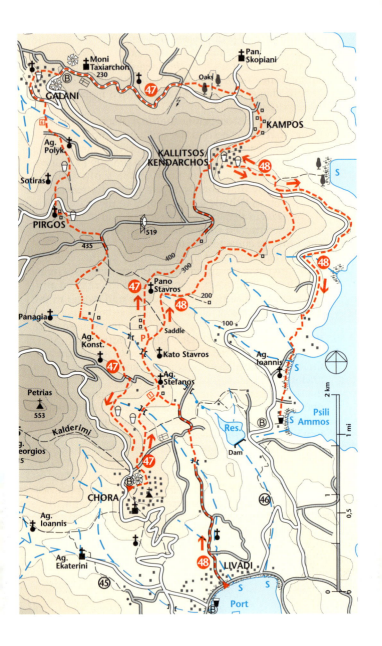

176 Sérifos

🔴48 Kallítsos, the prettiest village

This five-hour walk on the unspoiled eastern side of the island leads along old, yet easily identifiable tracks to Kéndarchos, also called Kallítsos, "prettiest village".
Although the ascents are not too steep, the way there is, at 11 km, quite a challenge. Once there, you could take a bus or taxi back (see below). Psilí Ammos strand is the only place with tavernas, so food for the journey is a must. Kallítsos has two wells.
■ *11 km, difference in altitude 250 m, moderate*

▷ *Map see left*

AWT 0.00 From the middle of **Livádi** strand, 50 m to the right of the **restaurant ΣΤΑΜΑΤΗΣ** next to the sign "Amalia", a dirt road runs inland. We follow it, Chóra away above us on
0.10 the left, as far as a **hollow** covered with reeds and with two dovecotes (right). Immediately after them you go left up along concrete, pass a large holiday house on the left and head for the hill crowned by rocks resembling ruins.
0.20 Beneath this hill is a **bridge** beside more dovecotes 1.
It now takes eight minutes along a mule track to reach a dirt track, which you follow up to the right and, *already*
0.30 *after 40 m, left*. On the **crest** of the hill are a few houses – 46 crosses here. 100 m before a bridge in the next valley you are relieved to discover an almost forgotten monopáti at the end of the ridge. This track leads left up to a fork beside a ruin, where you go right (red-and-white marking "1", also the route of 47).

Livádi – Kalitsos – Psili Ammos

	On the next hilltop, beside a dirt track, are a house and
0.40	**St. Stephen's chapel**. In the next little green valley are a
0.45	solitary chapel on the right and further down a **bridge** with *curved steel railings*. Beyond the following, deeply sunken path our route leaves that of ㊼, which leads left up to Stavrós chapel (**P:** N 37°10,111'/ E 24°30,402').

	To the left of a wire mesh fence you go *straight ahead* and
0.55	come – latterly on a monopáti – to a **saddle** (245 m) with a fine view over Psilí Ammos bathing bay. More about that later.

You now descend to the right through a gorge covered with oleander bushes, directly beneath the antenna ②.

	The panorama extends from Sífnos as far distant Páros.
!!	
1.10	Do *not* take the path right down towards the sea at a **fork**, but continue straight ahead, keeping to the contour lines and partly without a path. Soon you go through a gully, then through bizarre boulders, always heading for the distant slopes.
1.20	On the right-hand side of the first foothill is a **hut** (250 m), after the second one you can look down into the Kéndarchos valley. The high-lying village of Kallítsos ③ was built to be safe from marauding pirates. The unplastered houses at that time were stone-grey and therefore hardly visible from the sea.
1.35	Further down the path joins the **road** near the power line. Cross it 40 m over to the left and then use a fairly wide dirt track for about 40 m downhill. At a reddish lump of rock you take a few steps up to the left and a footpath leading right, which forks after 150 m. To the right you could reach Kéndarchos pebble beach ④ in ten minutes. Keeping to the left, you soon approach the village and

discover a wayside well with clear water, the former washing place. From there it is only a few steps on up to beautiful **Kéndarchos/Kallítsos**. The main alley here also has a well and an inviting resting place. Kallítsos means: "the most beautiful village". Even so only a handful of inhabitants have stayed in the village.

1.55

2.10 We return past the washing place to the **road**. As this now covers the former path, and the terrain here is rather strenuous, we just have to make do with it. We proceed on the left side of the crash-barrier, imagining it is a dry-stone wall. Over to the left in the sea is the offshore island Vous ("ox's head").

2.25 Having gone round several bends, you come to **farmhouses** on the left directly beside the road. Immediately beyond them, to the right of a real dry-stone wall, you find a path running downhill. Shortly afterwards you have to surmount the wall in order to continue downhill. Alongside houses on the right, and then on a monopáti, you proceed to the valley bottom. Across the stream-bed

2.40 with thick vegetation you go left to reach **Agios Ioánnis** strand – a lot less busy than in Psilí Ammos, but without any tavernas.

From the end of the sandy beach you come to the hilltop

2.50 on the peninsula, making your way down to the **Psilí Ammos** beach by keeping to the right of the holiday complex. The name signifies "fine sand", which is plentiful here, not to mention tamarisks and two tavernas. And the bus to Livádi. At 16.50, 17.50, 18.50, ?? Sigá, sigá. (The tireless can also go on, see page 171.)

Livádi – Kalitsos – Psili Ammos   179

Síkinos

This island in the southern Cyclades consists of a marble massif overlain with slate. It is supplied with sufficient water from a number of springs.
Long overlooked by tourism, the island is gradually catching up, now possessing numerous well appointed rooms in addition to the fair-sized selection of harbour tavernas.
Thanks to the map of the island from Anavási, which is available everywhere, the hiker has no difficulty in finding his way around. Most of the original mule tracks are preserved, because the 240 permanent inhabitants are also content with fewer new roads: a trekking island of the highest order, walks 49 and 50 are specially recommended.

㊾ A lonely path

Not a soul in sight for a couple of hours ... Anyone keen to have such an experience will find regions behind Kástro and Apáno Chório where neither man nor beast will cross their path.
From Kástro (= AWT 1.05) the shortened tour takes five hours, from Aloprónia six to seven. The route almost entirely follows old monopátia. You can stop in Kástro, or later at a good well.
While this is one of the most impressive walks on the islands, it does require certain path-finding skills.
■ *12 km, difference in altitude 410 m, difficult*

AWT	In **Aloprónia** you go up the road from the **bridge** at the
0.00	strand to the petrol station, then up right towards Pirgári and further up until you reach the right-hand bend in the road. On the left is the reservoir, and to the right of it begins a rocky monopáti. Climbing gradually, it passes
0.20	**barns** (left) below a chapel. Further on is a well on the right-hand side. At the top of the mountain, in your direction of movement, is the large monastery.
0.40	Having crossed the road, use a small section of path through the ditch, but return to the **road** again. But you only use this for 60 m, as a dirt track commences to the left of the antenna. First dropping slowly, it then rises to
0.50	the charmingly furnished **Blasius Chapel**.
1.05	Here begins a mule track which runs uphill to the right of the ditch, goes round a bend and ends at wide steps leading up to **Kástro bus stop**. On the right is the last chance to do any shopping in Kástro.
1.10	The rest of the tour starts to the left of the chapel which you passed on your way up. Steps lead up to the "upper village", **Apáno Chório**. At the chapel on the lower outskirts you go up right through the sleepy, tightly clustered village.

At the end of the village you find another stair-path, which affords views of the sea on the other side of the island. A whole group of islands, dominated by Zeus, the highest peak on Náxos. At 1004 m, also the highest in the Cyclades.

1.20	The upper part of the village consists entirely of the ruins of houses. Ascending the steps between these, you stumble over the round stump of a **windmill**.

Behind it the old trail leads on up in the direction of the Paraskeví chapel at the top of the mountain. But you go right at the fork below that. Life is difficult enough as it is without having to slog up to the chapel as well.

1.30	Instead we relish the wonderful path which meanders along the side of the slope and brings us to the deserted hamlet **Stamatiní** (**P:** N 36°41. 318'/ E 25°06.463'). Going round the lowest house, you go downhill at the fork, soon sighting a double chapel ①. Ignore the turn-off to the
1.40	right, but not the **well** on the left a little further on, with its crystal-clear water.

Twenty metres beyond that you turn right at the fork on the slabs of rock and go downhill. A magnificent rock

path now begins ②. Over to the left on the counterslope a deserted settlement, down in the valley round cisterns. The trail follows the contours, ascending gradually.

As might be expected in such a bleak region, you discover
2.05 a round **refuge** further up and later, below a huge cairn, a
2.10 **second refuge** (**P:** N 36°40.713′/ E 25°07.218′).

Over towards the sea rises a cone-shaped mountain (379 m) whose right-hand slopes we will later use for the descent. On the slopes you pass a large round stone pen and to the right of it you come to a track which keeps left above the valley.

Quite far down in the valley you later come across some
2.35 **ruined houses** by the wayside. Soon after you notice a small house on the left-hand side on the counterslope. To the right above our track stands a dry-stone wall (**P:**
!! N 36°39.849′/E 25°07.171′). *Here you turn left down into the*
2.45 *valley bottom*. (You can tell you have gone too far and have to turn back if you see the Panteleimon chapel on your right after three minutes.)

Climbing up the other side of the valley, you pass a dried-up well on the left and walk straight on, later going through a cleft in the rock. Over on the right on the oppo-
3.00 site slope stands the Panteleimon chapel. From the **saddle** you then see the port of Aloprónia again. From there down you stroll across broad terraced cornfields until you
3.20 come to a **dirt track** which leads you effortlessly along the
3.35 shoreline to **Aloprónia**.

Another path from Aloprónia to Kástro.
Beside the apse of Panagía church (㊾, AWT 0.25) starts a path which first runs past a well and then – somewhat overgrown – through an amazing rocky landscape. Having crossed a hollow, you drop down to a valley with a sand track and on the other side find a stairway leading steeply uphill. 80 m below the stone huts keep left on the wide paved track, which then narrows to a monopáti and runs across the mountain ridge. After traversing a wide hollow with olive groves and a small canyon, we see our destination higher up, Kástro, to which several trails lead. (See ALT on the map)

50 Our Lady's Church in the temple

This eight-hour circular tour from Aloprónia leads to the island's most important archaeological site – a Roman marble sepulchral temple –, which is sadly closed. But it also has a few landscape highlights in store. Particularly enchanting is the initial stretch as far as Heróon temple, which the locals call Episkopí.
Walking almost entirely on mule tracks, we pass a number of wells, albeit sometimes without a pail. On the return leg between Manali's well and the sea you will require certain path-finding skills. If you start in Kástro, the trek can be reduced by 1.5 hours.
■ *17 km, difference in altitude 390 m, difficult*

▷ Map as far as AWT 0.25 on previous page

Short cut: Taking the **bus** as far as **Kástro**, you go up the steps to **Apáno Chorió** from the bus stop on the left of the chapel. In front of the first church you go straight ahead, then up the steps to the right as far as the next church (right). From here you always leave one row of houses between yourself and the fields on the left. At the end of the village you find steps leading on to a mule track and the point where a monopáti leads up above the Agios Stephános chapel (= AWT 1.15). Walking time to that point is 15 min.

AWT 0.00 If you wish to walk from **Aloprónia**, go 80 m up the road from the long bridge at the strand and turn on to a dirt track leading steeply up to the left.

184 Síkinos

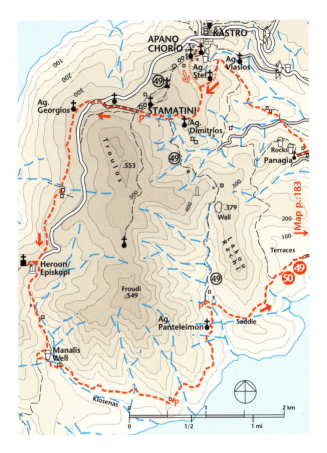

0.15   ***Short cut:*** After 15 minutes you could turn off to the right on to a track and make a short cut.

Otherwise you later disregard a turn-off to the left and come further up, after ruins and a field wall, to the de-
0.25   lightfully situated **Panagía Church** overlooking the harbour ①.

Walk back 150 m from the church until you find a path going to the left *in front of the field wall*. This takes you in-
0.35   to the **valley**, across a sandy track and up the other side, on the left-hand side of rocky ledges. At the top you reach an old mule track which first runs on the flat, then uphill

Aloprónia – Kastro – Episkopí – South Coast – Aloprónia

	through a charming, typically Greek landscape until it
0.55	joins a **horizontal path**.
!!	Go right here, turning *left after a small house (right)* on to
1.00	a path **leading uphill** between high walls. This path later peters out, though, so you climb up to Agios Stephános chapel without a path – but find another there. At the top
1.15	you come to a **monopáti** running along the side of the hill and go left. (You would have come from the right had you taken the short cut from Kástro.)
	At the next fork you go up right, at the next one straight
1.20	ahead and then down to the solitary **Agios Dimítrios chapel**, a nice spot for a picnic. Further down is an ill de-
1.25	fined **fork**, where walk 49 drops down to the left – today we go up to the right and after a few metres pass a well (right). Now go uphill, straight ahead at the turn-off to
1.35	the left, to the deserted hamlet **Stamatiní**.
	True monopátists will be reluctant, but here we have to
!!	hike on tracks *below the mule track* until we reach a dirt
1.40	track which ends at the **road**. Go left up it for 100 m, where a large sign indicates the "old path"; we gladly fol-
1.45	low this and soon come to the **St. George's chapel**.
	We now ramble up and down between abandoned terraced cornfields, Folégandros to our right. Be sure to take time to sit down every now and again and savour the
★	landscape ②. There follows a descent into a ditch with a
2.05	turn-off, but you go uphill and pass some **ruins** (left), between which a path leads uphill.
2.15	Here you proceed straight ahead, then climb again. **Below the road** are markings to the right which lead you along a monopáti, appropriately enough, to Heróon – al-
2.20	so called **Episkopí** ③.

3000 years ago this lonely region was the site of an ancient Ionian city, whose acropolis stood on the mountain now crowned by the Agía Marína chapel. Down here were the necropolises, the most important of which was the Heróon, the marble tomb of a noble family; two crypts still remain. In the 5th century AD it was converted into Our Lady's Church, integrating the ground plan and the entrance façade into the new structure. In 1688 the church became Episkopí monastery, whose cells and embrasures are still partly preserved.

Coming away from this impressive place, you return along the familiar path for 200 m, but then turn right downhill. Instead of schist you soon feel marble slabs beneath your feet ④. Up to the right of the path stands a

2.35
2.50 **small house**. Describing a right-hand bend round the mountain, the path eventually brings you to **Manali's well**.

Further down, after two or three minutes, you come to a
!! slab of rock, from where you go *left* through a small wall and then across the valley. After passing the ruins of some houses (right), you proceed along rather overgrown
!! tracks, *keeping to the left of the valley bottom*, towards the sea. Be careful not to lose sight of the trail!

At the sea (**P:** N 36°39.210'/ E 25°06.732') the path turns
3.25 off to the left 15 m below some **ruins**. Again it starts off rather overgrown. You pass a tall rocky needle (right) and,
3.50 round the bend, come to **Agios Panteleímon chapel**, which provides a "divine" resting place.

Continuing on along the slope, you go right after three or four minutes (**P:** N 36°39.849'/ E 25°07.171'), down into
3.55 the **valley bottom**. This corresponds to AWT 2.45 on
4.50 walk 49. Now follow that description as far as **Aloprónia**.

▶ **Lodging at the waterside** is possible at the delightful pension Lucas in Aloprónia (tel. 22860 51076)

Aloprónia – Kastro – Episkopí – South Coast – Aloprónia 187

🛈 Naval review

This pleasant, three-hour walk through charming scenery leads along marvellous mule tracks and ends up at the famous monastery Zoodóchos Pigí, the monastery of the "life-giving source". Along the way hikers can also refresh themselves at a real source.

■ *11 km, difference in altitude 80 m, moderate*

AWT 0.00 — Starting point is the obelisk on the Platía in **Kástro**. The closely interlocking medieval Venetian kástro used to stand here, but was pulled down by the Italian occupying forces during the war.

Proceed along the left-hand side of the church, then left into the next alleyway and past the Café Posto (left). Continue strolling straight ahead on the flat and turn right into an alley with a chapel on the left ①. Behind it steps lead up left to the monastery – we stay on the horizontal paved track and leave the village to the right with a cheerful heart.

0.15 — At the fork above the antenna you go left, with views over to the island Ios, until you reach the road near **Agios Modestos chapel**, with barrel-vaulted roof.

Take the road up as far as the turn-off to the helicopter pad. On the dirt track which follows you do not go straight ahead, but down to the right and later straight on past the football field (right). Hard to imagine 22 players fitting on to that for the island's big local derby.

0.25 — Having left the wide, ascending dirt track **to the right**, you follow a path above an olive grove (right). Ahead of

188   Síkinos

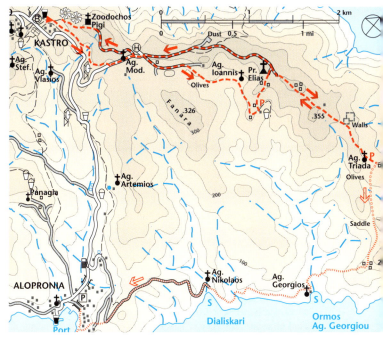

you lies a simply gorgeous, lonely trail above terraced cornfields. Soon you can pick out the Elias chapel on the mountain, our first destination. Down in the valley you later pass the St. John's chapel ②, from where the path takes a left sweep round the mountain upon which the Elias chapel stands. Now you should watch out:

0.45 When descending, you see a **small house** on the right be-
!! low the trail (**P:** N 36°42.198'/ E 25°08.858'). A few metres before actually reaching the house, you notice *indistinct tracks* heading uphill to the left. Follow these, climbing to the right of a dry wall. (If you are thirsty, stay on the trail, go left past the house and make for a well a little further down.)

At the end of the ascent you go past some ruins before
1.00 coming to the **Profítis Elias chapel**. The splendid view rewards you for your efforts.

From there tracks lead over to a dirt track. In front of us the Cycladic islands are laid out like a naval fleet. On the

Kástro – Agía Triáda – Zoodóchos Pigí – Kástro 189

★	left Mílos, then Antíparos, Páros, Náxos with the highest Cycladic peak, Zeus, to the right of it Iraklía and many more.
	One really ought to delight in the regal spectacle a little longer before proceeding to the right and taking the
1.10	monopáti in front of a quarry. Later it runs through a **hollow**, where it temporarily becomes a well-beaten track. Fi-
1.25	nally it leads you alongside a very long dry wall to **Agía Triáda Chapel** ③. (P: N 36°42.400'/ E 25°09.665').

Alternative: If you have the Anavási map with you, you might head down to the very beautiful sandy beach of **Agios Geórgios**. The only drawback is that the paths depicted there hardly exist, which means that you have to hike without a path for a further two-and-a-half hours before reaching Aloprónia again along the coast. And there are (unfortunately) plans afoot to build a coast road.

1.50	The less strenuous option is to walk back to the **Elias chapel** and hoof it down the roadway from there. Moving along above the steep coastline, you again command a view of the neighbouring islands (your own naval review), making you quite overlook the rubbish dump.
	The roadway veers inland, once more passing the heli-
2.15	copter pad. Immediately after that you take the **sandy track up to the right** and come past the well-fortified
2.25	rear of the deserted **fortified monastery of Zoodóchos Pigí** ④, perched mightily on the rock above the sea. You
2.30	skip down the old steps leading to **Kástro**, regretting the imminent dilapidation of the windmills.

A ship will come ...

The most pleasant way to travel through the world of the Greek islands is on the large and inexpensive ferries, with plenty of space on the upper deck for taking the sea air. The terrible series of shipping accidents in the year 2000, EU safety regulations and foreign competition have resulted in technical upgrades and better training of the crews on the ferryboats. In recent years the fast catamarans have captured the lion's share of the market. Unfortunately one can seldom sit in the open air in these floating waiting rooms, besides they are much more expensive. Be sure to book your passage before summer weekends, for otherwise they often only offer space in the pricey VIP class. The obsolete "Flying Dolphins" have all but disappeared.

Upon arriving at Athens airport, you can pick up timetables for the following days from the Greek National Tourism Organization. You can sail both from Piraeus and from Lávrion near Athens, although the latter has nowhere to stay overnight.

The main route of the big ferry services, usually with frequent daily sailings, begins in Piraeus and continues via Kíthnos, Sérifos, Sífnos, and occasionally Kímolos to Mílos. The catamarans ply the same route, but not via Kíthnos and Kímolos.

From Mílos it is not always possible to reach Santoríni every day, so it is sometimes preferable to take the east route from Athens via Páros. In the south Cyclades the leisurely "Nissos Thira" – along with less frequent ferries – serves Folégandros, Síkinos, Ios, Santoríni and Anáfi.

Inter-island connections away from main routes can be made by using small ferries, such as for example between Mílos and Kímolos as well as between Santoríni and Thirassía. Boats sail several times a day to Kéa from the mainland port of Lávrion, less frequently from Kíthnos.

Those wishing to push on out to the east Cyclades can choose between services from Kíthnos and Sérifos several times a week as well as daily sailings from Santoríni and Ios.

Current timetables on the internet:

Ferries:	www.bluestarferries.com www.ventouris.gr www.gaferries.gr www.minoan.gr www.lane.gr www.forthnet.gr www.gtpnet.com
Fast boats:	www.hellenicseaways.gr www.aegeanspeedlines.gr www.superfast.com www.dolphins.gr

Abbreviations, Key

	hiking route on a road or dirt track
	hiking route on a street
	hiking route on a path
	hiking route without a path
ALT	alternative route, short cut
← ⇐	walking direction/alternative
P	GPS point
	street
	dirt road, sandy track
MP	monopáti, mule track
	dry stream-bed (at times), hollow
	antenna
Ⓑ ⁞Ḃ⁞	bus stop/seasonal
Ⓟ	parking area
Ⓗ	helicopter landing pad
	cemetery
+	wayside shrine, monument
	sports field
∩	cave
	medieval castle, dwelling tower / ruins
	ancient ruins, statue
▪ ▫	houses/ruins
	monastery, large church/ruins
	chapel/summit chapel/ruins
	taverna/open seasonally
	windmill, ruins
	fountain, well, spring, reservoir, cistern
S	swimming possible

In the text:

!!	pay attention to turn-off!
	possible feelings of vertigo
OW	time for walking one way
★	the author's 20 favourite spots